The Wisdom of
W.E.B. DU BOIS

Also available from The Wisdom Library

THE WISDOM OF JOHN ADAMS
THE WISDOM OF BUDDHA
THE WISDOM OF CONFUCIUS
THE WISDOM OF GEORGE ELIOT
THE WISDOM OF SIGMUND FREUD
THE WISDOM OF GANDHI
THE WISDOM OF GIBRAN
THE WISDOM OF CARL JUNG
THE WISDOM OF THE KABBALAH
THE WISDOM OF OMAR KHAYYAM
THE WISDOM OF THE KORAN
THE WISDOM OF MAO
THE WISDOM OF KARL MARX
THE WISDOM OF MUHAMMAD
THE WISDOM OF THEODORE ROOSEVELT
THE WISDOM OF BERTRAND RUSSELL
THE WISDOM OF THE SAINTS
THE WISDOM OF SARTRE
THE WISDOM OF SHAKESPEARE
THE WISDOM OF THE TALMUD
THE WISDOM OF THOREAU
THE WISDOM OF LEO TOLSTOY
THE WISDOM OF THE TORAH
THE WISDOM OF OSCAR WILDE

Published by Citadel Press

The Wisdom of

W.E.B. DU BOIS

EDITED BY ABERJHANI

PHILOSOPHICAL LIBRARY

CITADEL PRESS
Kensington Publishing Corp.
www.kensingtonbooks.com

To Wallace Edward Lloyd, Sr., for exceptional demonstrations of love, strength, and wisdom.

And to Michael Porter, for honoring and extending the Du Bois tradition of cultivating human potential and steadfastly speaking Truth to Power.

CONTENTS

ACKNOWLEDGMENTS

Expressing gratitude to Stephany Evans and Richard Ember for entrusting and blessing me with this, their beautiful brainchild.

And to John Earnest Carpenter, Jr.: Ships without anchors stand little chance of surviving the hurricane season; thanks for remaining one of my anchors.

INTRODUCTION

I am one who tells the truth and exposes evil and seeks with
Beauty for Beauty to set the world right.
—W. E. B. Du Bois

In the year that W. E. B. Du Bois was born, 1868, black elected officials in a South undergoing reconstruction used their newly gained legislative powers to begin a battle for the unimpeded civil rights and educational advancement of African Americans. That same year, the U.S. Congress passed the Fourteenth Amendment to the Constitution, confirming the citizenship of "all persons born or naturalized in the United States," and reinforcing for African Americans the foundation of freedom established only a few years earlier by Abraham Lincoln's Emancipation Proclamation and the Thirteenth Amendment. In the year that Du Bois died, 1963, one hundred years after the Emancipation Proclamation was issued, a quarter of a million black and white Americans converged on Washington, D.C., in an effort to conclude the battle begun in 1868, and that Du Bois waged his entire life.

It is not too much to imagine that upon his birth on February 23, 1868, Du Bois was baptized and branded in the flames of political debate that obscured the recent past, sought to define the present, and fought to mold the future. In his efforts to confront and correct the most destructive social and political issues of his time, W. E. B. Du Bois lived a rare, extremely courageous, and exceptionally committed life. Often dismayed by but generally unflinching in the face of perpetual adversity, he engaged the battle for equal human rights and for modern civilization itself as an educator, literary artist, international statesman (albeit one without official U.S. government sanction), and perhaps above all else, as an evolved spiritual being capable of at once fiercely excoriating his enemies with unrelenting condemnation and gently embracing them with fraternal compassion. For him, Booker T. Washington was not the oversimplified accommodationist of historical essays, but a leader whose principle failure was a lack of insight into the balance required between the individual integrity of black laborers and the political integrity of a predominantly white society. For him, the Ku Klux Klan represented not just an organization of hooded terrorists, but rather a group of people as oppressed by ignorance and America's failure to eradicate racism as struggling blacks were.

Looked at through the windows of the past while standing firm in the cross-cultural currents of the present, the issues can appear exaggerated, inane, and at times terrifyingly surrealistic. Such issues as suffrage for African Americans and women; the apartheid system of segregation sentimentally referred to as Jim Crow; the hyper-real practice of genocide by lynching; and what Du Bois perceived of as a basic imbalance in the quality of life experienced between America's haves and have-nots, were authenticated by history and validated by the divine potential of human beings to rise above such barbaric ignominy. What was less justifiable or excusable was not just one race's basic assumption of superiority over another, but its apparently heartfelt belief that the "other" was not even human. That belief, Du Bois often pointed out, had led to all manner of social, political, sexual, and spiritual abuses, not the least of which, he felt, was that visited upon the heads of the oppressor rather than the oppressed. How was the darker brother to convince his lighter-hued kin that he was genuinely human and not some clever species of animal capable of aping human qualities? How was he to prove that whatever chains of despair or destiny bound one also bound the other? As blatantly preposterous as the debate over the humanity of blacks may seem now—a debate waged in popular magazines, scientific journals, lecture halls, churches, and the U.S. Congress—defenders of it were no less adamant or unapologetic in their beliefs then, than those proponents of eugenics who continue to champion similar beliefs in the modern era.

In the ninety-five years that composed his life, Du Bois never stopped fashioning the tools necessary to construct the bridges so crucial to relations between men and women, between the ignorant and the educated, the ideal of freedom and the application of democracy, between blacks and whites, whites and themselves, and blacks and themselves. His efforts to bridge these gaps started long before his contribution to the founding of the National Association For the Advancement of Colored People (NAACP) in 1910 and his legendary tenure as editor of the *Crisis: A Record of the Darker Races*. As early as 1897, he had already joined intellectual and spiritual forces with the dynamic educator and Episcopalian minister Alexander Crummell in the founding of the American Negro Academy, and in 1900 pledged himself to the ideals of global black unity at the first Pan African Congress, led by the Trinidadian Henry Sylvester Williams in London. His publication of *The Souls of Black Folk* in 1903 represented less an attack on the social philosophies of Booker T. Washington than the eloquent expansion and evolution of Washington's indispensable accomplishments. Each of these achievements represented a weighted move to obliterate the propaganda that blacks were subhuman anomalies and to foster the ideal of the black, white, brown, and yellow races as one great human race.

Even with the founding of the seemingly militant Niagara Movement in 1905, the call was for an end to apartheid in America so that democracy might truly flourish and establish a genuine spiritual complement to America's technological advances of the late 1800s and early 1900s. Should not the people who built the gleaming towers and speeding trains of Chicago and New York City cultivate characters equal to the beauty and wonder of their creations? As it was, the Niagara Movement provided a political springboard for the establishment and eventual success of the NAACP. The NAACP in turn provided Du Bois with the editorship of *Crisis* magazine for more than two decades— the closest he would come to an official public office. Through the *Crisis*, he monitored and addressed the policies of one U.S. president after another, not just on matters pertaining to race but on those regarding war, the precarious ethics leading to the precarious economics of Wall Street, neo-colonialism, and the general state of the union. And along with James Weldon Johnson, Alain Locke, and Charles S. Johnson, he provided the drive, focus, and means for the phenomenal success of the celebrated Harlem Renaissance. Moreover, while he wrangled with the larger issues that shaped the destinies of nations via editorials and lectures and conventions, he could also make time to acknowledge in a letter such "smaller" issues as a father seeking advice on what books to buy for his children, or his own daughter's contentment with the activities of her day.

The passion with which Du Bois gave himself to the struggle for human rights might seem to counter the fact that he was an avowed pacifist. Nevertheless, while he was not one who hungered for violent conflict, he did believe that, when confronted with it, one was obligated to seek resolution. As he stated in *Crisis* magazine in January, 1912: "I am resolved to be quiet and law abiding, but to refuse to cringe in body or in soul, to resent deliberate insult, and to assert my just rights in the face of wanton aggression."

The organizational tools with which Du Bois fought his battles for humanity were many, including a series of Pan African Congresses on several different continents, affiliations with the Peace Information Center in New York City, the Communist Party, and the American Labor Party. But possibly none of these served quite so well as his own prolific and penetrating writings. His collected works, compiled following his death, came to some three dozen volumes incorporating every literary genre: letters, essays, poetry, speeches, plays, novels, and history. Whereas *The Souls of Black Folk* made him famous in 1903, he had in fact already confirmed the seriousness of his intellectual intent with the 1896 publication of *The Suppression of the African Slave-Trade to the United States of America, 1638–1870,* and the 1899 publication of his classic sociological study, *The Philadelphia Negro.* His first novel, *The Quest of the Silver Fleece,* came in 1911. The essay collections *Darkwater* and *The Gift of Black Folk* appeared in 1920 and 1924 respectively, while one of his confessed favorite books, the novel *Dark Princess,* was published at the height of the Harlem Renaissance in 1928. With the Great Depression came his masterful revisionist history, 1935's *Black Reconstruction in America, 1860–1880,* followed by *Black Folk: Then and Now* in 1939 and *Dusk of Dawn: an Autobiography of a Concept of Race* in 1940.

The above are but examples of an exhaustive stream of writings. The more than considerable power of his pen never failed Du Bois. Even under excruciating persecution at the hands of the Joseph McCarthy–led House Committee on Un-American Activities in the 1950s, the wealth of his genius overflowed with fictional trilogies, articles, and biography. Right up until his death in Ghana in 1963, he labored to give form to a treasured vision: his proposed multi-volume *Encyclopaedia Africana*. As massive an under-taking as Du Bois's encyclopedia was, a version of it would not see completion until three decades later when advanced communications and computer technology provided schol-ars Kwame Anthony Appiah and Henry Louis Gates, Jr., with the means to publish *Africana: The Encyclopedia of the African and African American Experience*, dedicated to Du Bois and Nelson Rolihlahla Mandela.

Among the many battles that Du Bois fought in his war to affirm dignity and equality for African Americans and all human beings, was one with publishers who would change his capitalization of the word "Negro" to the lower-cased "negro" in his articles. For Du Bois, the distinction was more spiritual and political than grammatical or stylistic. Free Afri-can Americans who during American slavery advocated for the freedom of other blacks and took every precaution to ensure their own, disassociated themselves from the word "negro" because it was also applicable to slaves. They were not slaves, and in an era when all blacks were supposedly free, Du Bois insisted that editors and publishers recognize that fact by retaining his use of the word "Negro" spelled with a capital "N." In honor of his struggle to endow that word with the substance of racial dignity, political equality, and historical truth, his use of the word "Negro" has been retained in this volume of quotations.

The words of wisdom, warning, compassion, joy, and hopefulness offered by W. E. B. Du Bois in the pages that follow are remarkable for their ability to articulate the es-sential challenges of his own age while illuminating the plight of the modern, and, indeed, virtually every known historical era. He was at once a scientist in his skillful use of history as a tool for comprehending the present, and a prophet in the application of his gift for analyzing the pre-sent as an indicator of the future. Because he lived both firmly entrenched within his time and decades ahead of it, the light of his wisdom, like that of his great love for humanity, is one that never diminishes.

—Aberjhani
Savannah, Georgia

Civilization and Human Nature

Surpassing the notion of an historical concept or social theory, civilization represented for W.E.B. Du Bois an obtainable spiritual ideal. Key to that ideal in the early twentieth century was the ability and willingness of men and women from different races and cultural backgrounds to recognize the opportunity that history had placed before them through a confluence of unique events, trends, and circumstances. Modern democracy in the United States, spurred on by revolutions in Europe and Cuba and Africa, afforded Americans an opportunity to construct a society unprecedented in its potential to provide common citizens the advantages of freedom, prosperity, and privilege enjoyed only by the elite in most civilizations. Moreover, rapid advances in communication and transportation were making the world smaller and smaller every day, so that whatever benefited the United States might well benefit the rest of the world.

However, the ultimate test of this new opportunity was not how efficiently businessmen capitalized on financial contingencies or how cleverly politicians managed to garner power and influence. Nor was it even the safeguarding of citizens' rights on behalf of the common woman and man. The ultimate test came with the desire of those who would govern a civilization and those who would inhabit one to abandon all pretense to social superiority and bow in loving service before one another.

As life in general constituted much pain in the form of struggles against poverty, disease, ignorance, and emotional anguish, what more civilized way for people to alleviate the same than by giving themselves to one another as brothers and sisters in deed as well as in word? A society of people hoping to become politically superior needed first to become spiritually valid.

The ultimate test on the way to establishing an ideal civilization encouraging ideal human behavior was to look bravely beyond gender, color, ethnic origin, religious difference, and class distinctions to discover and honor the value of each unique individual. The possibility was a universal one, capable of operating within any governmental setting or system. Obviously, democracy or any other form of government as a shared spiritual vision was something that would not be easily achieved. The question became a matter of each individual's willingness to recognize the possibility and embrace the challenge. Moreover, the endeavor could not stop with the efforts of a single nation. True civilization would never register as true civilization until it became, regardless of political or religious division, the motivating standard of all people in all nations.

It remains a big vision—some would certainly say laughable—for the world to entertain. It is the kind of goal that deprives humanity of any choice between "the Dream of the Spirit or the Pain of the Bone" and forces all to confront both.

———————————

In the civilized world each serves all, and all serve each, and the binding force is faith and skill, and the skill is bounded only by human possibility and genius, and the faith is faithful even to the untrue.

The battle for humanity is not lost or losing.

Which is really Truth—Fact or Fancy? the Dream of the Spirit or the Pain of the Bone?

The most hopeless of deaths is the death of Faith.

All this life and love and strife and failure—is it the twilight of nightfall or the flush of some faint-dawning day?

Herein lies the tragedy of the age: not that men are poor—all men know something of poverty; not that men are wicked—who is good? Not that men are ignorant—what is Truth? Nay, but that men know so little of men.

Thicken the thunder of God's voice, and lo! a world awakes!

Human unity within and without Nations, must and will succeed.

Nations reel and stagger on their way; they make hideous mistakes; they commit frightful wrongs; they do great and beautiful things.

Human advancement is not a mere question of almsgiving, but rather of sympathy and cooperation among classes who would scorn charity.

Men have forgotten where civilization started.

How hard a thing is life to the lowly, and yet how human and real.

Civilization must show two things: the glory and beauty of creating life and the need and duty of power and intelligence.

Feeling like dying isn't going to help things a bit.

The Valley of the Shadow of Death gives few of its pilgrims back to the world.

It is wrong to encourage a man or a people in evil-doing; it is wrong to aid and abet a national crime simply because it is unpopular not to do so.

The matter of our logic is not nearly so important as that of our ethics and religion.

Let the ears of a guilty people tingle with truth.

To increase abiding satisfaction for the mass of our people, someone must sacrifice something of his own happiness. This is duty only to those who recognize it as a duty.

It is a hard thing to live haunted by the ghost of an untrue dream.

"Wed with truth" . . . dwell above the veil.

Inspiration strives with doubt, and faith with vain questionings.

The scars and foibles and contradictions of the Great do not diminish but enhance the worth and meaning of their upward struggle; it was the bloody sweat that proved the human Christ divine; it was his true history and antecedents that proved Abraham Lincoln a Prince of Men.

Let us follow the clear light and afterward turn to other darknesses.

With clean hands and honest hearts we must front high heaven and beg peace in our time.

From the use of insult grows the arrogant, overbearing nation which so often blindly misses the way of truth; from the bigotry of persecution grows the dead rot of mental death, and from war and murder come national as well as individual death.

Every man owes a certain respect to his own soul.

The roots of the tree, rather than the leaves, are the sources of its life.

Still this widening of the idea of common Humanity is of slow growth and to-day but dimly realized.

There is always a certain glamour about the idea of a nation rising up to crush an evil simply because it is wrong.

The oblivion of complete surrender or of complete silence. The object of life is to avoid either of these.

How can love of humanity appeal as a motive to nations whose love of luxury is built on the inhuman exploitation of human beings, and who, especially in recent years, have been taught to regard these human beings as inhuman?

The greatest satisfaction comes from the sacrifice of to-day's enjoyment that tomorrow's may be greater.

Make yourself do unpleasant things, so as to gain the upper hand of your soul.

One has a terrible plunge to make into some lurking pool of life.

The main thing is the YOU beneath the clothes and skin—the ability to do, the will to conquer, the determination to understand and know this great, wonderful, curious world.

A pious belief outweighs an impious unbelief.

World philanthropy, like national philanthropy, must come as uplift and prevention and not merely as alleviation and religious conversion.

We strive for this broader vision of peace and good will.

A new standard of national efficiency is coming. And that efficiency is marked by the way in which a great modern advanced nation can be neighborly to the rest of the world.

Let the world take no backward step in that slow but sure progress which has successively refused to let the spirit of class, of caste, of privilege, or of birth, debar from life, liberty, and the pursuit of happiness a striving human soul.

The place of those who would ride the conflagration is truly within and not behind or in front of the Holocaust.

Back of it all, back of the flesh, the mold, the dust, there must be Reality.

Woe to the man, who, with the revelation of the world once before him, as it stands before you now, has let it fade and whiten into common day—life is death.

Without infinite life, life is a joke and a contradiction.

Humanity is progressing toward an ideal; but not, please God, solely by help of men who sit in cloistered ease, hesitate from action and seek sweetness and light; rather we progress to-day, as in the past, by the soul-torn strength of those who can never sit still and silent while the disinherited and the damned clog our gutters and gasp their lives out on our front porches.

A true and worthy ideal frees and uplifts a people; a false ideal imprisons and lowers.

Whenever a community seats itself helplessly before a dangerous public desire, or an ingrained prejudice, recognizing clearly its evil, but saying, "we must cater to it simply because it exists," it is final; change is impossible. Beware; the epitaph of that people is being written.

When you have chosen, stand by it, for the man who ever is wavering and choosing again is wasting God's time.

It is not the things which people have that makes the major part of civilization—the real civilization; real culture depends on quality and not quantity.

When in other days the world lied, it was to a world that expected lies and consciously defended them; when the world lies today it is to a world that pretends to be true.

What human reform demands today is light, more light; clear thought, accurate knowledge, careful distinctions.

It is the highest optimism to bring forward the dark side of any human picture.

Evolution is evolving the millenium, but one of the unescapable factors in evolution are the men who hate wickedness and oppression with perfect hatred, who will not equivocate, will not excuse, and will be heard.

Being a problem is a strange experience—peculiar even for one who has never been anything else, save perhaps in babyhood and in Europe.

We deliberately and continuously deceive not simply others, but ourselves as to the truth about them, us, and the world.

We still yield the well-born the advantages of birth, we still see that each nation has its dangerous flock of fools and rascals; but we also find most men have brains to be cultivated and souls to be saved.

The insistent problem of human happiness is still with us.

Only the soul that suffers knows its suffering. Only the one who needs knows what need means.

Human nature is not simple and any classification that roughly divides men into good and bad, superior and inferior, slave and free, is and must be ludicrously untrue and universally dangerous as a permanent exhaustive classification.

His revolt was against things unsuitable, ill adjusted, and in bad taste; the illogical lack of fundamental harmony; the unnecessary dirt and waste—the ugliness of it all—that revolted him.

We can afford the Truth.

It is certain that all human striving must recognize the hard limits of natural law, and that any striving, no matter how intense and earnest, which is against the constitutions of the world, is vain.

Religious ideals have always far outrun their very human devotees.

The world is shrinking together; it is finding itself neighbor to itself in strange, almost magic degree.

Who shall restore to men the glory of sunsets and the peace of quiet sleep?

Doubtless, and in the long run, the greatest human development is going to take place under experiences of widest human contact.

Everybody is in favor of justice so long as it costs them no effort.

The alternative of not dying like hogs is not that of dying or killing like snarling dogs. It is rather, conquering the world by thought and brain and plan; by expression and organized cultural ideals.

Pessimism is cowardice.

To lay any class of weak and despised people, be they white, black, or blue, at the political mercy of their stronger, richer, and more resourceful fellows, is a temptation which human nature seldom has withstood and seldom will withstand.

Not by guarding the weak in weakness do we gain strength, but by making weakness free and strong.

Deception is the natural defense of the weak against the strong.

It is an awful thing to have to be ashamed of one's self.

What shall the end be? The world-old and fearful things— war and wealth, murder and luxury? Or shall it be a new thing—a new peace and a new democracy of all races—a great humanity of equal men?

2

Women

To Mary Silvina Burghardt Du Bois, W.E.B. Du Bois was a devoted son. To Nina Gormand, and after her death, to Shirley Graham, he was a loving husband. To Nina Yolande (as well as to Burghardt Gomer, his son who died in infancy) he was a proud and doting father. As a son, husband, and father, Du Bois engaged a perspective on women not endorsed by the majority of men of his era. He was a feminist who lobbied for the social, political, and sexual equality of women. Like that of his contemporary, Ida B. Wells Barnett, his political agenda placed the urgency of securing civil rights for African Americans a notch above that of obtaining the same for women in general, but he never let it drift far from the sphere of his concerns.

The issue for Du Bois was as much a matter of political and social practicality as it was one of sacred duty. As the son of a nomadic father, Alfred Du Bois, who left his family when Du Bois was still a toddler, he was very much aware of the limitations placed upon the lives of women by their forced dependence on men. The painful irony was that in cases like that of his mother, women were often forced to accept the responsibilities refused by men but were left without the social or economic means to meet those responsibilities. American women, like so many others around the world, were trained largely to live as second-class citizens, and living as a second-class citizen meant living as a victim. It was only by empowering them with full social and economic equality that average mothers, wives, and daughters of the world stood a chance of providing for themselves and the offspring they bore.

Most extreme among the abuses of women were those suffered by black women during American slavery. Against their will, they served in turn as instruments of sexual pleasure for their white masters and as breeding mares for the institution of slavery. Added to the shock of the routine violation of their bodies was the trauma of having to relinquish their children to unknown slave-holders. Du Bois considered this physical, mental, and spiritual abuse of black women—with its inevitable result being the destruction of the traditional African family—the highest crime committed by slave-holders and the one thing for which he said he could not forgive them. In his universe, the image of the black mother was that of a sacred being whose innate enchantment had been polluted and diluted by the ignorance, greed, and lust of white men. She now "sobbed her life away in song, longing for her lost palm trees and scented waters." Many of his writings were offered as atonement for the ignored tears of mothers, wives, and daughters.

All religion, from beauty to beast, lies on her eager breasts; her body bears the stars, while her shoulders are necklaced by the dragon.

No state can be strong which excludes from its expressed wisdom, the knowledge possessed by mothers, wives and daughters.

There was a day in the world when it was considered that by marriage a woman lost all her individuality as a human soul and simply became a machine for making men. We have outgrown that idea.

God send us a world with woman's freedom and married motherhood inextricably wed.

In other years women's way was clear: to be beautiful, to be petted, to bear children. Such has been their theoretic destiny and if perchance they have been ugly, hurt, and barren, that has been forgotten with studied silence.

We cannot abolish the new economic freedom of women. We cannot imprison women again in a home or require them all on pain of death to be muses and housekeepers.

The uplift of women is next to the problem of the color line and the peace movement, our greatest modern cause.

Not being expected to be merely ornamental, they have girded themselves for work, instead of adorning their bodies only for play. Their sturdier minds have concluded that if a woman be clean, healthy, and educated, she is as pleasing as God wills and far more useful than most of her sisters.

The church is woman.

Your mother is Kali, the Black one; wife of Siva, Mother of the World.

It is inconceivable that any person looking upon the accomplishments of women today in every field of endeavor, realizing their humiliating handicap and the astonishing prejudices which they face and yet seeing despite this that in government, in the professions, in sciences, art and literature and the industries they are leading and dominating forces and growing in power as their emancipation grows—

it is inconceivable that any fair-minded person could for a moment talk about a "weaker" sex.

My mother and I were good chums. I liked her.

It is the mother I ever recall,—the little far off mother of my grandmothers, who sobbed her life away in song, longing for her lost palm trees and scented waters; the tall and bronzen grandmother, with beaked nose and shrewish eyes, who loved and scolded her black and laughing husband as he smoked lazily in his high oak chair; above all, my own mother, with all her soft brownness.

The statement that woman is weaker than man is sheer rot: it is the same sort of thing that we hear about "darker races" and "lower classes."

The world still wants to ask that a woman primarily be pretty and if she is not the mob points and asks querulously, "What else are women for?"

That a man should cheat, lie, steal, and seduce women, was to Sammy's mind almost normal; that he should tell the truth, give away his money, and stick by his wife was also at times probable.

The actual work of the world today depends more largely upon women than upon men.

Other things being equal, all of us, black and white, would prefer to be beautiful in face and form and suitably clothed; but most of us are not so, and one of the mightiest revolts of the [twentieth] century is against the devilish decree that no woman is a woman who is not by present standards a beautiful woman.

Twenty centuries before Christ a great cloud swept over seas and settled on Africa, darkening and well-nigh blotting out the culture of the land of Egypt. For half a thousand years it rested there, until a black woman, Queen Nefertari, "the most venerated figure in Egyptian history," rose to the throne of the Pharoahs and redeemed the world and her people.

For this, their promise, and for their hard past, I honor the women of my race.

They came first, in earlier days, like foam flashing on dark, silent waters—bits of stern, dark womanhood here and there tossed almost carelessly aloft to the world's notice. First and naturally they assumed the panoply of the ancient African mother of men, strong and black, whose very nature beat back the wilderness of oppression and contempt.

The world that wills to worship women studiously forgets its darker sisters.

Perhaps even higher than strength and art loom human sympathy and sacrifice as characteristic of Negro womanhood.

The meaning of the twentieth century is the freeing of the individual soul; the soul longest in slavery and still in the most disgusting and indefensible slavery is the soul of womanhood.

3

Love, Art, and Culture

In the Du Boisian universe, art and culture assumed their value from the roles to which they were assigned and eventually played in a given society. Art, rightly applied, provided humanity with the symbols, insight, and vicarious experience necessary to help one person place him- or herself in the shoes of another, and by so doing come to appreciate the commonality of human experience. It also provided the essential tools by which humanity elevated itself from those baser instincts promoting bloodlust and xenophobia to higher inclinations for the sustenance of intellectual and spiritual interaction, cultivation and evolution of the self, and the maintenance of a moral value system that both defined and perpetuated civilized conduct on a large scale.

Likewise, the beauty of culture came not so much from artifacts as from the "little courtesies" of everyday behavior. It was by the grace of mutual respect and acknowledgment rather than by the rareness of a painting one possessed or the exclusiveness of one's membership in a club that indicated a refined sensibility. One's intelligence was indicated by nothing quite so much as one's ability to recognize and appreciate the activities of divine purpose from within the "lowest" of society's laboring masses to the "highest" of its dynastic elite.

Bereft of consciously applied constructive goals, art and culture tended to glorify the potentially worst in any given society or individual. Beauty degenerated to decadence, grace to greed, and freedom to the enslavement of one's senses to a material world run amok. As a forerunner of and major contributor to the Harlem Renaissance of the 1920s and 1930s, Du Bois helped shape the sensibilities of a generation of poets, playwrights, painters, sculptors, and composers to make them wary of art's alluring pitfalls.

Even in its weakest form—that of emotional infatuation—love was something superior to both art and culture. In the face of a world where economic hardships often ground the best of the human spirit into the worst, love provided a pathway into hidden chambers of the spirit where nobility and compassion might be salvaged, resurrected, and made stronger. Before the thunderous clamor of political debate or war set loose in the world, love insisted on its promise for the possibility of human unity: between men and women, between blacks and whites, northerners and southerners, haves and have-nots, self and self. Its power and its value and its terror lay in its ability to dominate with joy all other aspects of reality. It was the one thing for which all else—political conviction, art, culture, self-respect, even power—might justifiably be sacrificed because it was the one thing capable of transforming chaos into hope.

Love is eternal spring. Life lifts itself out of the winter of death. Children sing in mud and rain and wind. Earth climbs aloft and sits astride the weeping skies.

Gentle culture and the beauty and courtesies of life—they are the real end of all living.

Art is not simply works of art; it is the spirit that knows Beauty, that has music in its soul and the color of sunsets in its headkerchiefs; that can dance on a flaming world and make the world dance, too.

Love-songs are scarce and fall into two categories—the frivolous and light, and the sad. Of deep successful love there is ominous silence.

The thinkers, dreamers, poets of the world must be its workers. Work is God.

The tools of the artist in times gone by? First of all, he has use of the Truth—not for the sake of truth, not as a scientist seeking truth, but as one upon whom Truth eternally thrusts itself as the highest handmaid of imagination, as the one great vehicle of universal understanding. Again artists have used Goodness—goodness in all its aspects of justice, honor, and right—not for sake of an ethical sanction but as the one true method of gaining sympathy and human interest.

Marriage stopped secret longings and wild open revolt. It solved the woman problem once and for all.

What was marriage? . . . It came to mean for her a litter of children, poverty, a drunken, cruel companion, sickness and death. Why?

All art is propaganda and ever must be, despite the wailing of the purists.

If beauty were to become a standard of survival how small our world population would be!

We have had a score of artists and poets in black America, but few critics dared call them so.

Art is long, but industry is longer.

The object of satire is to point out fault and evil by the very exaggeration of its fun; and the test of its genuineness is its honesty and clearness of object.

Beauty? What is it?

Such is Beauty. Its variety is infinite, its possibility is endless. In normal life all may have it and have it yet again.

They that walked in the darkness sang songs in the olden days—Sorrow Songs—for they were weary at heart.

Whenever two human beings of any nation or race desire each other in marriage, the denial of their legal right to marry is not simply wrong—it is lewd.

To do in science and literature to-day anything worth the doing, anything that is really good and lasting, is hard to anyone, impossible to many.

The world of black folk will some day arise and point to Jean Toomer as a writer who first dared to emancipate the colored world from the conventions of sex.

The price of culture is a lie.

The culture indigenous to a country, its folk-customs, its art, all this must have free scope or there is no such thing as freedom for the world.

New artists have got to fight their way to freedom.

Through all the sorrow of the Sorrow Songs there breathes a hope—a faith in the ultimate justice of things.

It [love] rises from the ecstasy of our bodies to the communion of saints, the resurrection of the spirit, and the exquisite crucifixion of God. It is the greatest thing in our world.

A great song arose, the loveliest thing born this side the seas. It was a new song. It did not come from Africa, though the dark throb and beat of that Ancient of Days was in it and through it. It did not come from white America—never from so pale and hard and thin a thing, however deep these vulgar and surrounding tones had driven. Not the Indies nor the hot South, the cold East or heavy West made that music. It was a new song and its deep and plaintive beauty, its great cadences and wild appeal wailed, throbbed and thundered on the world's ears with a message seldom voiced by man. It swelled and blossomed like incense, improvised and born anew out of an age long past, and weaving into its texture the old and new melodies in word and in thought.

They sneered at it—those white Southerners who heard it and never understood. They raped and defiled it—those white Northerners who listened without ears. Yet it lived and grew; always it grew and swelled and lived, and it sits today at the right hand of God, as America's one real gift to beauty; as slavery's one redemption, distilled from the dross of its dung.

4

Freedom and Democracy

The population of the United States at the turn of the twentieth century was estimated at some 100,000,000 people consisting of the descendants of English settlers, the offspring of former slaves, immigrants from throughout Europe, and refugees from all over the world. Many embraced the United States as the ultimate haven of political freedom and the most promising experiment in democracy the world had ever seen. The metaphorical description of the country as a melting pot was apt enough but one that implied, erroneously thought some, that each ethnic group making its way to the United States eventually lost its more distinct features in a mixture of cross-cultural and cross-racial variables. Du Bois was more inclined to view this melting pot from the perspective of an idea later popularized as the salad bowl concept, which proposed that each group retained its individual characteristics while both absorbing and sharing traits with other groups. This then allowed each to enhance the cultural experience of the other and in the process strengthening the ideal and practice of democracy for all.

The concept of a government by the people and for the people was one Du Bois took very much to heart. In his role as the founder of the Niagara Movement and later as one of the principal founders of the NAACP, he did more than articulate social criticism. He exemplified democracy in action and challenged the limitations that a society prone to racism attempted to place upon his freedom as an African American and as an individual. Participating in a succession of Pan African Congresses, first held in London in 1900 and re-established in Paris following World War I, he presented himself as a U.S. delegate and world citizen attempting to secure democracy and freedom for people of color throughout the world.

More than one student of the historian and sociologist's life observed that Du Bois's character and bearing reflected that of a president or prime minister and theorized that had he been white, his destiny would indeed have led him to a governorship or presidency. Certainly his compassion for people from every background, his many intellectual gifts, and his natural flair for leadership placed him on par with founding fathers like Thomas Jefferson and John Quincy Adams. Ideologically, he picked up where the founding fathers left off by addressing issues and aspects of democracy still considered radical a century later. Questions such as the extent to which ordinary citizens should determine their own salaries or exercise direct authority, or "real power," went too far beyond the comfort zone of most political thinkers. Nevertheless, it was only by posing the hard questions and addressing the difficult issues pertaining to democracy that people in the United States could ever come to truly experience freedom.

That Du Bois adopted communism and moved to Ghana at the end of his life is one of his most powerful political statements. Being the educator that he was, it's possible he did not intend this action to encourage an abandonment of democracy in America at all, but that he employed the gesture to advocate a more vigorous and sincere application of democracy in his homeland.

The rich world is wide enough for all, wants all, needs all.

We may as well ask in the beginning: Just what does one mean by equality?

Only Talent served from the great Reservoir of All Men of All Races, of All Classes, of All Ages, of Both Sexes—this is real Aristocracy, real Democracy—the only path to that great and final Freedom which you so well call Divine Anarchy.

Political power today is but the weapon to force economic power. Tomorrow, it may give us spiritual vision and artistic sensibility.

Difference, either physical or spiritual, does not argue weakness or inferiority.

Human beings are infinite in variety, and when they are agglutinated in groups, great and small, the groups differ as though they, too, had integrating souls. But they have not. The soul is still individual if it is free; the group is a social, sometimes an historical fact.

Democracy is not a gift of power, but a reservoir of knowledge.

There is in this world no such force as the force of a man determined to rise.

We merely pause to ask: What is democracy anyhow?

Oppression is oppression. It is our privilege in the world to relieve it.

It is to be expected that every new voting class and every

new democracy will make its costly and ridiculous mistakes— will pass through demagoguery, extravagance, "boss" rule, bribery and the like; but it is through such experiences that voters learn to rule and the cost although vast is not excessive if the end is finally gained.

The cost of liberty is less than the price of repression.

Protest is for two purposes: first, for its effect upon your political enemies, and secondly, for its effect upon yourself.

Freedom has come to mean not individual caprice or aberration but social self-realization in an endless chain of selves, and freedom for such development is not the denial but the central assertion of the revolutionary theory.

Democracy in determining income is the next inevitable step to democracy in political power.

There is no power under God's high heaven that can stop the advance of eight thousand thousand honest, earnest, inspired and united people.

Democracy is not an end; it is a method of aristocracy.

One cannot, to be sure, demand of whole nations exceptional moral foresight and heroism; but a certain hard common-sense in facing the complicated phenomena of political life must be expected in every progressive people.

A republic must be based upon universal suffrage or it is not a republic.

What can be more instructive than the leadership of a group

within a group?—that curious double movement where real progress may be negative and actual advance be relative retrogression. All this is the social student's inspiration and despair.

The test of any great movement toward social reform is the excluded class.

The battle we wage is not for ourselves alone but for all true Americans. It is a fight for ideals, lest this, our common fatherland, false to its founding, become in truth the land of the thief and the home of the slave.

All social growth means a succession of social problems.

America early became a refuge for religion—a place of mighty spaces and glorious physical and mental freedom where silent men might sit and think quietly of God and his world.

The soul, long pent up and dwarfed, suddenly expands in new-found freedom.

It is easy for us to lose ourselves in details in endeavoring to grasp and comprehend the real condition of a mass of human beings. We often forget that each unit in the mass is a throbbing human soul.

Only democratic government can be both enlightened and selfish, both bond and free.

Dishonesty in public life has no monopoly of time or place in America.

Honest and earnest criticism from those whose interests are

most nearly touched,—criticism of writers by readers, of government by those governed, of leaders by those led,—this is the soul of democracy and the safeguard of modern society.

What we ought to do in America is to seek to bind the races together rather than to accentuate differences.

We are facing today still the elementary problem of democracy: How far do we dare trust the mass of the people, not with sham power and sounding phrases, but with real power?

Responsibility without power is a mockery and a farce.

All social struggle is evidenced by the rise, first of economic, then of social classes, among a homogenous population.

The class struggle of exploiter and exploited is a reality.

Agitation is a necessary evil to tell of the ills of the Suffering. Without it many a nation has been lulled to false security and preened itself with virtues it did not possess.

More and more clearly a splendid ideal flamed in the minds of Americans. This was to be a land of refuge and a land of freedom.

The present problem of problems is nothing more than democracy beating itself helplessly against the color bar.

The essence of social democracy is that there shall be no excluded or exploited classes in the socialistic state; that there shall be no man or woman so poor, ignorant or black as not to count one.

Within and without the somber veil of color vast social forces have been at work,—efforts for human betterment, movements toward disintegration and despair, tragedies and comedies in social and economic life, and a swaying and lifting and sinking of human hearts which have made this land [America] a land of mingled sorrow and joy, of change and excitement and unrest.

What we have on earth is men. Shall we help or hinder them? Shall we hate and kill them or love and preserve and uplift them?

To be a poor man is hard, but to be a poor race in a land of dollars is the very bottom of hardships.

Democracy is a method of doing the impossible. It is the only method yet discovered of making the education and development of all men a matter of all men's desperate desire.

Sometimes the so-considered minor problem is so tremendous and insistent that it leaps to the fore and demands examination and honest facing. This is particularly so when we have not simply ignored the problem but have deliberately and cynically lied about it, denied it, and said not that "Social Equality" was not a pertinent and pressing problem; but rather that it was no problem at all.

The human soul cannot be permanently chained.

Democracy alone is the method of storing the whole experience of the race for the benefit of the future, and if democracy tries to exclude women or Negroes or the poor or any

class because of innate characteristics which do not inter-
fere with intelligence then that democracy cripples itself
and belies its name.

It is the awful penalty of injustice and oppression to breed
in the oppressed the desire to oppress others.

Agitation does not mean Aggravation—Aggravation calls
for Agitation in order that Remedy may be found.

The method of entrusting the government of a people to a
strong ruler has great advantages when the ruler combines
strength with ability, unselfish devotion to the public good,
and knowledge of what that good calls for.

The broader the basics of democracy the surer is the universal appeal for justice to win ultimate hearing and sympathy.

A rising group of people are not lifted bodily from the
ground like an inert solid mass, but rather stretch upward
like a living plant with its roots still clinging in the mould.

Intelligence in voting is the only real support for democracy.

The hushing of the criticism of honest opponents is a dangerous thing.

Discriminating and broad-minded criticism is what the South
needs—needs it for the sake of her own white sons and
daughters, and for the insurance of robust, healthy mental
and moral development.

Equality of opportunity for unbounded future attainment is
the rightful demand of mankind.

Democracy is a method of realizing the broadest measure of justice to all human beings.

Only by putting power in the hands of each inhabitant can we hope to approximate in the ultimate use of that power the greatest good to the greatest number.

Most philosophers see the ship of state launched on the broad irresistible tide of democracy, with only delaying eddies here and there; others, looking closer, are more disturbed.

The cure for the ills of democracy is seen to be more democracy.

The best and most effective aristocracy, like the best monarchy, suffered from lack of knowledge; they did not know or understand the needs of the people, and they could not find out, for in the last analysis only the man himself, however humble, knows his own condition.

The rise of a nation, the pressing forward of a social class, means a bitter struggle, a hard and soul-sickening battle with the world such as few of the more favored classes know or appreciate.

Lovers of democracy have declined to consider the possibility of the masses voting their own wages.

The great world now and then becomes aware of certain currents within itself—tragedies and comedies, movements of mind, gossip, personalities—in some inner whirlpool of which it had been scarcely aware before. Usually these things are of little interest or influence for the main current of events; and yet is not this same main current made up of the impinging of these smaller swirlings of little groups?

Social equality may mean two things. The obvious and clear meaning is the right of a human being to accept companionship with his fellow on terms of equal and reciprocal courtesy. . . . Social equality is [also] the right to demand private social companionship with another.

The real argument for democracy is then that in the people we have the real source of that endless life and unbounded wisdom which the real ruler of men must have.

The emancipation of man is the emancipation of labor and the emancipation of labor is the freeing of that basic majority of workers who are yellow, brown, and black.

The true significance of slavery in the United States to the whole social development of America lay in the ultimate relation of slaves to democracy. What were to be the limits of democratic control in the United States? If all labor, black as well as white, became free—were given schools and the right to vote—what control could or should be set to the power and action of these laborers? Was the rule of the mass of Americans to be unlimited, and the right to rule extended to all men regardless of race and color, or if not, what power of dictatorship and control; and how would property and privilege be protected? This was the great and primary question which was in the minds of the men who wrote the Constitution of the United States and continued in the minds of thinkers down through the slavery controversy. It still remains with the world as the problem of democracy expands and touches all races and nations.

Democracy died save in the hearts of black folks.

This [freedom] was the coming of the Lord. This was the fulfillment of prophecy and legend. It was the Golden Dawn, after chains of a thousand years. It was everything miraculous and perfect and promising.

And yet emancipation came not simply to black folk in 1863; to white Americans came slowly a new vision and a new uplift, a new sudden freeing of hateful mental shadows. At last democracy was to be justified of its own children.

America thus stepped forward in the first blossoming of the modern age and added to the Art of Beauty, gift of the Renaissance, and to Freedom of Belief, gift of Martin Luther and Leo X, a vision of democratic self-government: the domination of political life by the intelligent decision of free and self-sustaining men. What an idea and what an area for its realization—endless land of richest fertility, natural resources such as Earth seldom exhibited before, a population infinite in variety, of universal gift, burned in the fires of poverty and caste, yearning toward the Unknown God; and self-reliant pioneers, unafraid of man or devil.

So in blood and servile war, freedom came to America. What did it mean to men? The paradox of a democracy founded on slavery had at last been done away with. But it became more and more customary as time went on, to linger on and emphasize the freedom which emancipation brought to the masters, and later to the poor whites. On the other hand, strangely enough, not as much has been said of what freedom meant to the freed; of the sudden wave of glory that rose and burst above four million people, and of the echoing shout that brought joy to four hundred thousand fellows of African blood in the North.

The magnificent trumpet tones of Hebrew Scripture, transmuted and oddly changed, became a strange new gospel. All that was Beauty, all that was Love, all that was Truth, stood on the top of these mad mornings and sang with the stars. A great human sob shrieked in the wind, and tossed its tears upon the sea—free, free, free.

Democracy, that inevitable end of all government, faces eternal paradox. In all ages, the vast majority of men have been ignorant and poor, and any attempt to arm such classes with political power brings the question: Can Ignorance and Poverty rule? If they try to rule, their success in the nature of things must be halting and spasmodic, if not absolutely nil; and it must incur the criticism and raillery of the wise and the well-to-do. On the other hand, if the poor, unlettered toilers are given no political power, and are kept by exploitation in poverty, they will remain submerged unless rescued by revolution; and a philosophy will prevail, teaching that the submergence of the mass is inevitable and is on the whole best, not only for them, but for the ruling classes. In all this argument there is seldom a consideration of the possibility that the great mass of people may become intelligent, with incomes that insure a decent standard of living. In such case, no one could deny the right and inevitableness of democracy.

5

African Americans

Du Bois often expressed in his writings a great love for "the brotherhood of humanity" as a whole and recognized that the bloodlines of his ancestry flowed from several ethnic sources, including Dutch, French Huguenot, and African. Revering the notion that all nations constituted one large human family, he nevertheless professed as well that he reserved his deepest affections for African Americans.

While the enslavement of African Americans was an unavoidable historical fact, so was the historical record of their courage in the face of mortal danger, their strength before seemingly insurmountable odds, their faith when confronted with conditions that had driven others to hopeless despair, and their evocation of beauty and genius under oppressive circumstances that did not encourage either. Whether as field laborers, soldiers, inventors, surrogate parents to white charges, ministers, singers, carpenters, or journalists, African Americans had advanced the evolution of the United States even as they had quietly exalted themselves. Few were the places in history where one could point to the kind of unbridled cruelty and oppression suffered by African Americans in slavery. Fewer still were those places where one could find a race of people emerging out of such conditions with their capacity for joy, forgiveness, and love still intact.

With his early devotion to the publication of original works on African-American culture and history, Du Bois established, with Black History Week founder Carter G. Woodson later following his lead, the foundations for studies of black history and sociology in modern American academia. By doing so, he created a tradition to which scores of black scholars committed themselves and proudly extended from one generation to the next.

As his own generation grappled with the issues of Jim Crow segregation and the fundamental acceptance in American society of blacks as human beings, Du Bois believed it important to produce a work that would illustrate not only African American contributions to world culture and history but those of people of African descent all over the world. Such a book would serve as an important legacy for blacks and hopefully provide whites with insights to their darker brothers and sisters beyond their clearly myopic, prejudiced, and deadly misperceptions of them. Toward that end, he began as early as 1909 to formulate plans, identify resources, and communicate with others to produce an *Encyclopedia Africana*, a detailed multi-volume study of black life and history around the world produced by blacks around the world. It is a true testament to his genius that a book that he envisioned at the beginning of the twentieth century could not be completed until the end of the century when advancements in communications and computer technology allowed renowned scholars Kwame Anthony Appiah and Henry Louis Gates, Jr., to complete the project in the form a single 2,095-page volume.

Before the pilgrims landed we were here.

A certain spiritual joyousness; a sensuous, tropical love of life, in vivid contrast to the cool and cautious New England reason; a slow and dreadful conception of the universe, a drawling and slurring of speech, an intense sensitiveness to spiritual values—all these things and others like them, tell of the imprint of Africa on Europe in America.

Colored folk have much to remember and they will not forget.

Affirm as you have the right to affirm, that the Negro race is one of the great human races, inferior to none in its accomplishment and in its ability.

Character and brains were too much for prejudice.

Emancipated and given a vote, despite his ignorance and inexperience, he gave the South three gifts, so valuable that no one to-day would dream of giving them up: (1) The public-school system; (2) the enfranchisement of the poor whites; and (3) the beginning of modern social legislation in land reform, eleemosynary institutions, and social uplift.

Black Blood with us in America is a matter of spirit and not simply of flesh.

There grew up in the minds of the free Negro class a determination and a prejudice which has come down to our day. They fought bitterly with every means at their command against being classed with the mass of slaves. It was for this reason that they objected to being called Negroes. Negroes was synonymous with slaves. They were not slaves.

We American blacks are very common people. . . . We come out of the depths—the blood and mud of battle. And from just such depths . . . came most of the worth-while things in this old world.

What if the Negro people be wooed from a strife for right-eousness, from a love of knowing, to regard dollars as the be-all and end-all of life?

The religious growth of millions of men, even though they be slaves, cannot be without potent influence upon their contemporaries.

America has feared the coming forward of these black men; it has looked upon it as a sort of threat.

Bewildered we are, and passion-tost, mad with the mad-ness of a mobbed and mocked and murdered people.

A double life, with double thoughts, double duties, and double social classes, must give rise to double words and double ideals, and tempt the mind to pretence or revolt, to hypocrisy or radicalism.

After the Egyptian and Indian, the Greek and Roman, the Teuton and Mongolian, the Negro is a sort of seventh son, born with a veil, and gifted with a second sight in this American world,—a world which yields him no true self-consciousness, but only lets him see himself through the revelation of the other world. It is a peculiar sensation, this double-consciousness, this sense of always looking at one's self through the eyes of others, of measuring one's soul by the tape of a world that looks on in amused contempt and pity. One ever feels his twoness,—an American, a Negro; two souls, two thoughts, two un-reconciled strivings; two warring ideals in one dark body, whose dogged strength alone keeps it from being torn asunder.

From the double life every American Negro must live, as a

Negro and as an American, as swept on by the current of the nineteenth while yet struggling in the eddies of the fifteenth century—from this must arise a painful self-consciousness, an almost morbid sense of personality and a moral hesitancy which is fatal to self-confidence.

A tremendous striving group force is binding this group together, partly through the outer pounding of prejudice, partly by the growth of inner ideas. What they can and will do in the rebuilding of a better, bigger world is on God's knees and not now clear; but clarity dawns, and so far as we gain self-consciousness today we can be a force tomorrow.

What hurts us is the mere memory that any man of Negro descent was ever so cowardly as to despise any part of his own blood.

The blacker the mantle, the mightier the man! For blackness was ancient ere whiteness began.

A Negro by any other name would be just as black and just as white.

Biologically we are mingled of all conceivable elements, but race is psychology, not biology.; and psychologically we are a unified race with one history, one red memory and one revolt.

Throughout history, the powers of a single black man flash here and there, like falling stars, and die, sometimes before the world has rightly gauged their brightness.

The Negro is primarily an artist.

We cannot reverse history; we are subject to the same natural laws as other races, and if the Negro is ever to be a factor in the world's history—if among the gaily colored banners that deck the broad ramparts of civilization is to hang one uncompromising black, then it must be placed there by black hands, fashioned by black heads, and hallowed by the travail of 200,000,000 black hearts beating in one glad song of jubilee.

America knows the value of Negro labor.

The future world will, in all reasonable probability, be what colored men make it.

With the use of their political power, their power as consumers, and their brainpower, added to that chance of personal appeal which proximity and neighborhoods always give to human beings, Negroes can develop in the United States an economic nation within a nation, able to work through inner cooperation, to found its own institutions, to educate its genius, and at the same time, without mob violence or extremes of race hatred, to keep in helpful touch and cooperate with the mass of the nation.

The inability of the Negro to escape from a servile caste into political freedom turned the problems of the group into problems of family life.

The wretched of my race that line the alleys of the nation sit fatherless and unmothered.

The restoration and raising of home ideals must, then, come from social life among Negroes themselves.

We gained the right to fight for civilization at the cost of being Jim Crowed and insulted.

Our worst side has been so shamelessly emphasized that we are denying we have or ever had a worst side.

Those who do believe in men, who know what black men have done in human history, who have taken pains to follow even superficially the story of the rise of the Negro in Africa, the West Indies, and the Americas of our day know that our modern contempt of Negroes rests upon no scientific foundation worth a moment's attention. It is nothing more than a vicious habit of mind.

We refuse to kiss the hands that smite us.

Heredity is always stronger through the influence of acts and deeds and imitations than through actual blood descent; and the presence of the Negro in the United States quite apart from the mingling of blood has always strongly influenced the land.

Weighted with a heritage of moral iniquity from our past history, hard-pressed in the economic world by foreign immigrants and native prejudice, hated here, despised there, and pitied everywhere; our one haven of refuge is ourselves, and but one means of advance, our own belief in our great destiny, our own implicit trust in our ability and worth.

The black man that takes his medicine of insult, discourtesy, and prejudice sitting down and saying nothing, loses his own self-respect.

Our unrealized strength is so enormous that the world wonders at our stupid apathy.

There will be those who will want to say that the black race is the first and greatest of races, that its accomplishments are most extraordinary, that its desert is most obvious and its mistakes negligible. This is the kind of talk we hear from people with the superiority complex among the white and the yellow race.

American Negroes, to a much larger extent than they realize, are not only blood relatives to the West Indians but under deep obligations to them for many things.

[Marcus] Garvey is the beloved leader of tens of thousands of poor and bewildered people who have been cheated all their lives.

American Negro leaders are not jealous of Garvey—they are not envious of his success; they are simply afraid of his failure, for his failure would be theirs.

The sensation that Garvey created was due not so much to his program as to his processes of reasoning, his proposed methods of work, and the width of the stage upon which he essayed to play his part.

The role which the great Negro Toussaint, called L'Ouverture, played in the history of the Untied States has seldom been fully appreciated.

American Negroes will be beaten into submission and degradation if they merely wait unorganized to find someplace voluntarily given them in the new reconstruction of the economic world.

We are physically able to survive slavery, lynching, debauchery, mob-rule, cheating, and poverty, and yet remain the most prolific, original element in America, with good health and strength.

While the American officers were convinced of the Negro officers' incompetency and were besieging General Headquarters to remove them en masse, the French instructors at the Gondricourt Training School, where captains and selected lieutenants were sent for training, reported that the Negroes were among the best Americans sent there.

In some cases peasants and villagers were scared at the approach of Negro troops, but this was but temporary and the colored troops everywhere they went soon became easily the best liked of all foreign troops.

In practically every French town where the Negro troops stayed they left close and sympathetic friends among men, women, and children.

One cannot study the Negro in freedom and come to general conclusions about his destiny without knowing his history in slavery.

We are torn asunder within our own group because of the rasping pressure of the struggle without. We are as a race not simply dissatisfied, we are embodied dissatisfaction.

If the leading Negro classes cannot assume and bear the uplift of their own proletariat, they are doomed for all time.

The character of the Negro race is the best and greatest hope; for in its normal condition it is at once the strongest and the gentlest of the races of men.

Herein the longing of black men must have respect: the rich and bitter depth of their experience, the unknown treasures of their inner life, the strange readings of nature they have seen, may give the world new points of view and make their loving, living, and doing precious to all human hearts.

The main danger and the central question of the capitalistic development through which the Negro American group is forced to go is the question of the ultimate control of the capital which they must raise and use.

This agreement between capital and labor in regard to colored folk cannot be depended on.

They [blacks] of Atlanta turned resolutely toward the future; and that future held aloft vistas of purple and gold:— Atlanta, Queen of the cotton Kingdom; Atlanta, Gateway to the land of the Sun; Atlanta, the new Lachesis, spinner of web and woof for the world.

The black race is as vague for scientific definitions as the white.

When sticks and stones and beasts form the sole environment of a people, their attitude is largely one of determined opposition to and conquest of natural forces. But when to earth and brute is added an environment of men and ideas, then the attitude of the imprisoned group may take three mean forms—a feeling of revolt and revenge; an attempt to adjust all thought and action to the will of the greater group;

or, finally, determined effort at self-realization and self-development despite environing opinion. The influence of all these attitudes at various times can be traced in the history of the American Negro, and in the evolution of his successive leaders.

Fire and blood, prayer and sacrifice, have billowed over this people, and they have found peace only in the altars of the God of Right.

The development of the Negro church has been so extraordinary, and of such deep sociological interest that its future course is a matter of great concern.

In the Black World, the Preacher and teacher embodied once the ideals of this people—the strife for another and a juster world, the vague dream of righteousness, the mystery of knowing; but to-day the danger is that these ideals, with their simple beauty and weird inspiration, will suddenly sink to a question of cash and a lust for gold.

As bard, physician, judge, and priest, within the narrow limits allowed by the slave system, rose the Negro preacher, and under him the first Afro-American institution, the Negro church.

Our song, our toil, our cheer, and warning have been given to this nation in blood-brotherhood.

The question of the future is how best to keep these millions from brooding over the wrongs of the past and the difficulties of the present, so that all their energies may be bent toward a cheerful striving and cooperation with their white neighbors toward a larger, juster, and fuller future.

A belief in humanity is a belief in colored men. If the uplift of mankind must be done by men, then the destinies of this world will rest ultimately in the hands of darker nations.

Pushed aside as we have been in America, there has come to us not only a certain distaste for the tawdry and flamboyant but a vision of what the world could be if it were really a beautiful world; if we had the true spirit; if we had the Seeing Eye, the Cunning Hand, the Feeling Heart.

The study of Negro religion is not only a vital part of the history of the Negro in America, but an interesting part of American history.

Once in a while there flashes some clairvoyance, some clear idea, of what America really is. We who are dark can see America in a way that white Americans can not.

It was Negro loyalty and the Negro vote alone that restored the South to the Union; established the new democracy, both for white and black, and instituted the public schools.

The nation has not yet found peace from its sins; the freedman has not yet found in freedom his promised land. Whatever of good may have come in these years of change, the shadow of a deep disappointment rests upon the Negro people.

Would America have been America without her Negro people?

Beneath the veil lay right and wrong, vengeance and love, and sometimes throwing aside the veil, a soul of sweet Beauty and Truth stood revealed.

6

Education and Work

Education and productivity were cornerstones of the conservative New England Victorian culture and family environment in which Du Bois grew up. They were also two of the most crucial mainstays of social and political structure in the United States in general. The boom in public education following the Civil War combined with the increasing renown of such universities as Harvard in Cambridge, Massachusetts, and Columbia in New York City, had begun to modify the rugged pioneer character of the county's populace into one of some social polish, cultural sophistication, and political progressiveness. And the country's seemingly indefatigable spirit of industry and expansion had placed cities like Chicago and New York, with their towering skyscrapers and advanced transportation systems, among the world's first modern metropolitan centers.

Without access to the varied forms of education suitable for every individual temperament and every class of worker, the potential for continued growth and securing an authentically functional democracy in the United States decreased considerably. More than a means to a substantial paycheck, both education and satisfying work were the means to a substantial character. In the words of Du Bois, the purpose of education was not to make men carpenters, but to make carpenters men.

Ignorance, he would have the world know, was not an affliction restricted to a single race or class and he generally championed some form of higher education for all people, pointing out that poor southern whites and unschooled northern immigrants suffered as much from a lack of formal education as did the majority of African Americans at the time. Among the hallmarks of his many intellectual battles was an ongoing debate against Booker T. Washington's proposal that vocational training should comprise the dominant education allowed African Americans as a whole. Du Bois suggested vocational training for those with an aptitude for it and a secondary liberal arts education for those with an aptitude for it. In addition, in a rapidly advancing society like that of the United States, it would behoove even carpenters and farmers to acquire some measure of higher education on the way to their hammers and plows.

Whereas enlightenment by education was important for the stability and continued growth of the United States in general, it was essential for the "uplift" of African Americans in particular. Barely a generation out of slavery, forced servitude had not equipped blacks for the ordinary everyday responsibilities that went hand in hand with freedom. Their ultimate liberation could not stem from a presidential decree; it would have to come from the sense of self-possession and expanded awareness that only education could provide. Out of the larger group of educated blacks, Du Bois envisioned a Talented Tenth that would, by their individual gifts, strengths, and determination, further the advancement of their people and, by doing so, of the United States and humanity as a whole. This legion of informed and inspired black minds would penetrate all fields of endeavor, opening doors of opportunity formerly closed in business, science, the arts, politics, and the military.

For his own part, the renowned historian and sociologist remained a scholar and an educator all of his life. The setting of his classroom changed periodically, from a shack in the backwoods of Tennessee to the classes of Wilberforce University in Ohio and Atlanta University in Georgia. Whether as editor of *Crisis* magazine for two decades, as a guest lecturer in numerous halls across the United States and around the world, or as historian and champion of society's would-be underdogs, Du Bois taught the power of knowledge by absorbing it into the deepest channels of his own being, then joyfully dispersing it like seeds of essential hope. He demonstrated the power of knowledge by bravely living it every day of his adult life.

———————

Be honest, frank, and fearless and get some grasp of the real values of life.

After all, what is the object of life but human happiness and how far can and ought education to increase the sum of this happiness?

It is knowledge and cunning that are missing. Some know not and care not. Some know and care not. Some care not and know. We know and care, but, oh! how and where?

Men want work. They love work. Only give them the work they love and they will ask no pay but their own soul's "well done!"

The world must eat before it can think.

We are in a system of culture where disparity of income is such that respect for labor as labor cannot endure; where the emphasis and outlook is not what a man does but what he is able to get for doing it; where wealth despises work and the object of wealth is to escape work, and where the ideal is power without toil.

Education must not simply teach work—it must teach life.

The guiding of thought and the deft coordination of deed is at once the path of honor and humanity.

Patience, Humility, Manners, and Taste, common schools and kindergartens, industrial and technical schools, literature and tolerance—all these spring from knowledge and culture, the children of the university.

Intelligence, broad sympathy, knowledge of the world that was and is, and of the relation of men to it—this is the curriculum of that Higher Education which must underlie true life.

The object of all true education is not to make men carpenters, it is to make carpenters men.

Work is Heaven, Idleness Hell, and Wages is the "Well done!" of the Master who summoned all them that labor and are heavy laden, making no distinction between the black sweating cotton hands of Georgia and the First Families of Virginia, since all distinction not based on deed is devilish and not divine.

With the life work chosen, remember that it can become, as you will it, drudgery or heroism, prosaic or romantic, brutal or divine.

A really efficient workman must be today an intelligent man who has had good technical training in addition to thorough common school, and perhaps even higher training.

Thrift and toil and saving are the highways to new hopes and new possibilities.

The world will not give a decent living to the persons who are out to reform it.

There is the teacher, the giver of immortal life, the one who makes the child to start where the father left off, that the world may think on with one mind.

The method of the modern college has been proven by a hundred centuries of human experience: the importing of knowledge by the old to the young; the instilling of the conclusions of experience, "line upon line and precept upon precept."

Not a dream, but a mighty reality—a glimpse of the higher life, the broader possibilities of humanity, which is granted to the man who, amid the rush and roar of living, pauses four short years to learn what living really means.

College teachers cannot follow the medieval tradition of detached withdrawal from the world.

It is the trained living human, cultivated and strengthened by long study and thought, that breathes the real breath of life into boys and girls and makes them human, whether they be black or white, Greek, Russian, or American.

Teach thinkers to think—a needed knowledge in a day of loose and careless logic; and they whose lot is gravest must have the carefulest training to think aright.

Three universal laws underlie the necessity of earning a living; the law of work, the law of sacrifice, the law of service.

Inexperience can only be cured by experience.

The worker must work for the glory of his handiwork, not simply for pay; the thinker must think for truth, not for fame.

The vision of the rich meaning of life, which comes to . . . students, as men of culture, comes dimly or not at all to the plodding masses of men, and even to men of high estate it comes too often blurred and distorted by selfishness and greed.

Trained more and more to enjoy sexual freedom as undergraduates, we refuse as graduates to found and support even moderate families.

Our whole basis of knowledge is so relative and contingent that when we get to argue concerning ultimate reality and the real essence of life and the past and the future, we seem to be talking without real data and getting nowhere.

The eagerness to learn among American Negroes was exceptional in the case of a poor and recently emancipated folk. Usually, with a protective psychology, such degraded masses regard ignorance as natural and necessary, or even exalt their own traditional wisdom and discipline over "book learning"; or they assume that knowledge is for higher beings, and not for the "likes of us."

Had it not been for the Negro school and college, the Negro would, to all intents and purposes, have been driven back to slavery.

The Talented Tenth rises and pulls those that are worth the saving up to their vantage ground. This is the history of human progress; and the two historical mistakes which have hindered that progress were the thinking first that no more could ever rise save the few already risen; or second, that it would be better for the unrisen to pull the risen down.

The most useful and universal work, and the type of all other work, is that of the servant and common laborer.

All men cannot go to college but some men must.

Education and work are the levers to uplift a people. Work alone will not do it unless inspired by the right ideals and guided by intelligence.

And we serve first for the sake of serving—to develop our own powers, gain the mastery of this human machine, and come to the broadest deepest self-realization. And then we serve for the real end of service, to make life no narrow, selfish thing, but to let it sweep as sweeps the morning—broad and full and free for all men and all time, that you and I and all may earn a living and earn, too, much more than that—a life worth living.

It is the business of a modern government to see to it, *first*, that the number of the ignorant within its bounds is reduced to the very smallest number.

Either the United States will destroy ignorance or ignorance will destroy the United States.

Anyone who suggests by sneering at books and "literary courses" that the great heritage of human thought ought to be displaced simply for the reason of teaching the technique of modern industry is pitifully wrong and, if the comparison must be made, more wrong than the man who would sacrifice modern technique to the heritage of ancient thought.

The world today is trade: The world has turned shop-keeper.

Pay is simply the indication of present human appreciation of the work, but most of the world's best work has been, and is being done, unappreciated.

A simple healthy life on limited income is the only reasonable ideal of civilized folk.

Catholicity and tolerance, reason and forbearance can to-day make the world-old drama of human brotherhood approach realization; while bigotry and prejudice, emphasized race consciousness and force can repeat the awful history of the contact of nations and groups in the past.

Only that saner selfishness, which Education teaches, can find the rights of all in the whirl of work.

The test, then, of business is philanthropy; that is, the question as to how far business enterprise is doing for men the things they ought to have done for them, when we consider not simply their present desires, but their future welfare.

We have no right to sit silently by while the inevitable seeds are sown for a harvest of disaster to our children, black and white.

A friendly smile or pat will do wonders with even recalcitrant youth.

Names are only conventional signs for identifying things. Things are the reality that counts.

Every isolated group or nation must have its yeast, must have for the talented few centers of training where men are not so mystified and befuddled by the bard and necessary toil of earning a living, as to have no aim higher than their bellies, and no God greater than gold.

Ignorance is a cure for nothing.

The problem of education, then, among Negroes must first of all deal with the Talented Tenth; it is the problem of developing the Best of their race that they may guide the Mass away from the contamination and death of the Worst, in their own and other races.

The true college will ever have one goal—not to earn meat, but to know the end and aim of that life which meat nourishes.

Names are not merely matters of thought and reason; they are growths and habits.

There is far too much thoughtless toil and far too little knowledge of the material world among thinkers.

Names are nothing but little guideposts along the Way. The Way would be there and just as hard and just as long if there were no guideposts—but not quite as easily followed.

The public school should be a great democracy where all elements of the population come to realize the essential humanity of each.

The teachers, then, cannot be pedants or dilettantes, they cannot be more technicians and higher artisans, they have got to be asocial statesmen and statesmen of high order.

The history of civilization seems to prove that no group or Nation which seeks advancement and true development can despise or neglect the power of well-trained minds.

Common-school instruction in the South, in the modern sense of the term, was begun for Negroes by the Freedmen's Bureau and missionary societies, and the state public-school systems for all children were formed mainly by Negro Reconstruction governments.

The weakness of the Booker Washington philosophy was the assumption that economic power can be won and maintained without political power. The strength of the Washington philosophy was its insistence upon the necessity of manual labor, and its inculcation of thrift and labor.

Labor rather than gambling is the sure foundation of value and whatever we call it—exploitation, theft, or business acumen—there is something radically wrong with an industrial system that turns out simultaneously paupers and millionaires and sets a world starving because it has too much food.

The real owners of capital are small as well as large investors—workers who have deposits in savings banks and small holdings in stocks and bonds; families buying homes and purchasing commodities on installment; as well as the large and rich investors.

The laborer's equity is recognized, and his just share is a matter of time, intelligence, and skillful negotiation.

If we make money the object of man-training, we shall develop money-makers but not necessarily men; if we make technical skill the object of education, we possess artisans but not, in nature men. Men we shall have only as we make manhood the object of the work of the schools.

Education is that whole system of human training within and without the schoolhouse walls, which molds and develops men.

The riddle of existence is the college curriculum that was laid before the Pharoahs, that was taught in the groves by Plato, that formed the trivium and quadrivium.

Already in the smaller world, which now indirectly and anon directly must influence the larger for good or ill, the habit is forming of interpreting the world in dollars.

The function of the university is not simply to teach bread-winning, or to furnish teachers for the public schools or to be a centre of polite society; it is, above all, to be the organ of that fine adjustment between real life and the growing knowledge of life, an adjustment which forms the secret of civilization.

To-day we have climbed the heights where we would open at least the outer courts of knowledge to all, display its treasures to many, and select the few to whom its mystery of Truth is revealed.

They that do the world's work must do its thinking.

7

War and Revolution

Du Bois was born only three years after the conclusion of the Civil War, within a year that saw revolutions and invasions throughout Europe as well as the increasing military presence of Great Britain in Africa, most notably in Ethiopia. The Korean War was only ten years in the past when he died and the United States, emboldened by half a century of military conflicts and conquests around the globe, some far more costly than others, was just beginning its long inglorious march into the hell of the Vietnam war.

Throughout his long and fruitful ninety-five years of life, Du Bois bore witness to a succession of domestic and international conflicts that included revolutions, rebellions, scandalous alliances, even more scandalous betrayals, the comedy of bumbling espionage, and the tragedy of human butchery. Framed as his life was by all manner of political violence, war was not something Du Bois could view from a purely philosophical or historical distance. Wars and rumors thereof were very much a part of his teen and young adult years. He was thirty at the time of the Spanish-American War in 1898 and approaching forty at the time of the Russo-Japanese War in 1904 and the U.S. invasion of Cuba in 1906.

If he could have discerned in war a pragmatic advantage that furthered the development of enlightened civilization, Du Bois likely would have lent it his full support. And to a degree, in the case of the "Great War" known as World War I, he basically did because of the perceived threat to democracy and by extension the threat to the liberation of people of African descent around the world. With war having been engaged on such a titanic scale, there was, in truth, little else to do but lend one's support to one native land and people. For the most part, however, no matter the angle from which he might examine it, war came to one brutal paradox: a quest for peace and harmony in the name of mass murder.

The hard questions were forever Du Bois's favorites and in the case of war he offered a query that was extremely difficult primarily because it was extremely simple: as humanity claimed to desire peace and harmony above all else, why then did nations not prepare their industries to engage peace rather than war? Few viable answers have been forthcoming. Aware of the fear and distrust that curved rational considerations of war, Du Bois offered his own answer by allowing that pacifism was something he and Jesus Christ had very much in common.

Consider our chiefest industry—fighting.

The time must come when, great and pressing as change and betterment may be, they do not involve killing and hurting people.

First and foremost, war is war, and military organization is, and must be, tyranny. This is, perhaps, the greatest and most barbarous cost of war and the most pressing reason for its abolition from civilization.

Next to the abolition of war in modern civilization comes the regulation of birth by reason and common sense instead of by chance and ignorance.

The cause of war is preparation for war.

Here then comes the agitator. He is the herald—he is the prophet—he is the man that says to the world: There are veils which you do not know but which I know and you must listen to them.

It is quite possible that there have been times in the world when nothing but revolutions made way for progress.

The greater the international jealousies, the greater the corresponding costs of armament and the more difficult to fulfill the promises of industrial democracy in advanced countries.

In the awful cataclysm of World War, where from beating, slandering, and murdering us the white world turned temporarily aside to kill each other, we of the Darker Peoples looked on in mild amaze.

Whenever any nation allows impulse, whim or hasty conjecture to usurp the place of conscious, normative, intelligent action, it is in grave danger.

If we remember the history of all great reform movements, we remember that they have been preceded by agitation.

After the [Civil] war the sacrifice of Negro women for freedom and uplift is one of the finest chapters in their history.

It was this competition for the labor of yellow, brown, and black folks that was the cause of the World War. Other causes have been glibly given and other contributing causes there

doubtless were, but they were subsidiary and subordinate
to their vast quest for the dark world's wealth and toil.

Only within some great and all-inclusive empire or league
can separate nations and groups find freedom and protection and economic scope for development.

How easy and inevitable it is for an appeal to blood and
force to smash to utter negation any ideal for which it is
used.

Before the World War tendencies were strongly toward the
destruction of independent Africa, the industrial slavery of
the mass of the blacks and the encouragement of white immigration, where possible, to hold the blacks in subjection.

War and especially civil strife leave terrible wounds. It is
the duty of humanity to heal them.

A new, radical Negro spirit has been born in France, which
leaves us older radicals far behind. Thousands of young
black men have offered their lives for the Lilies of France
and they return ready to offer them again for the Sun-flowers
of Afro-America.

Eastward and westward storms are breaking,—great, ugly
whirlwinds of hatred and blood and cruelty. I will not believe them inevitable.

When the German host—grey, grim, irresistible, poured
through Belgium, out of Africa France called her sons; they
came; 280,000 black Senegalese, first and last—volunteers,
not drafted; they hurled the Boches back across the Durcy
and the Marne on a ghastly bridge of their own dead.

War is so tremendous and terrible a thing that only those who actually experience it can know its real meaning.

To some persons—to more human beings than ever before at one time in the world's history, there came during the Great War, during those terrible years of 1917 and 1918, a vision of the Glory of Sacrifice, a dream of a world greater, sweeter, more beautiful and more honest than ever before; a world without war, without poverty, and without hate.

People do not go to war for abstract theories of government. They fight for property and privilege.

Patient, loyal, intelligent, not grouchy, knowing all that they were up against among their countrymen as well as the enemy, those American black men won the war as perhaps no other set of S.O.S. men of any other race or army won it.

But for Black Africa, Germany would have overwhelmed France before American help was in sight. A tremendous wave of sentiment toward black folk welled up in the French heart.

War is murder.

As we saw the dead dimly through sifts of battle-smoke and heard faintly the cursings and accusations of blood brothers, we darker men said: This is not Europe gone mad; this is not aberration or insanity; this IS Europe; this seeming Terrible is the real soul of white culture—back of all culture—stripped and visible today.

The sole aim of any society is to settle its problems with its highest ideals.

We gained the right to fight for civilization at the cost of being "Jim Crowed" and insulted; we were segregated in the draft; we were segregated in the first officers' training camp; and we were allowed to volunteer only as servants in the Navy and as common laborers in the Army, outside of the four regular Negro regiments.

One must fight with his brains, if he has any.

It may be and often has been true that oppression and insult have become so intense and unremitting that there is no alternative left to self-respecting men but to herd by themselves in self-defense, until the attitude of the world changes.

The thing that we have got to face is that when for the sake of principle we take a radical position, we have got to pay for it.

To everyone war is, and, thank God, must be, disillusion.

I am a pacifist. So was Jesus Christ.

8

Whiteness and Race Relations

Growing up in the New England region of Great Barrington, Massachusetts, allowed Du Bois during his childhood to develop a personality unscarred by the psychologically debilitating effects of overt racism as it was practiced in other parts of the United States. It was not until he was ten years old that he became aware of life as something defined largely by the blackness of his skin—though it was much lighter than that of many darker African Americans—and the whiteness of his playmates'. That was when he found himself "shut out from their world by a vast veil" as a young white stranger, unlike his other playmates, refused to accept from him the greeting card they generally exchanged to announce an intent to visit their home. However, just as the event made him sensitive to his racial difference, it also forced him to recognize and rely upon his intellectual gifts to excel academically and refute the implied or stated charge that he was something inferior to anyone else.

Later, fortified and certified by one degree from Fisk University, studies in Berlin, Germany, and a Ph.D. from Harvard University, Du Bois dissected the conundrum of American race relations on every level. The impact of American slavery and the then ongoing practice of apartheid in the country had already demonstrated the devastating effects of the concepts of whiteness and blackness upon people of African descent. Within the American concept of race, blacks were political have-nots given to the command of whites because of their supposedly innate inferiority. If such inferiority was more a product of white imagination than black reality, the very real chains of forced servitude and the decades of oppression that followed had in fact made blacks economically and socially disadvantaged. The imagined inferiority was forced to become the truth in America just as it was in those African countries colonized by Europe.

What was less evident when weighing the cost of dividing human beings into categories of color was the consequences of such a practice upon whites. They were, Du Bois noted, many and devastating. For if the black family was continuously corroded by the economic and social instability generated by racism, the white family, particularly in the South, was often made incomplete by its need to deny and dehumanize offspring of mixed heritage. And if blacks suffered the degradation of knowing whites labeled them inferior, whites suffered the delusion with all its attendant mental and moral failings of believing the same.

Neither science nor history supported claims of inferiority and superiority. For whites to deny the humanity of black people was to deny their own humanity. Moreover, the claim to superiority was not new and it was nothing if not one vast psychological pitfall already writhing with history's dictators, despots, madmen, and bigots. What then were the implications of a national agenda with nothing more than the worship of whiteness as its principal goal? The way out of the maze of whiteness and blackness that led inevitably, repeatedly, to violent conflict was through the simple recognition of and respect for blacks and whites as not two races but one: the human race.

Sometime, somewhere, men will judge men by their souls and not by their skins.

The problem of the twentieth century is the problem of the color line, the question as to how far differences of race which show themselves chiefly in the color of the skin and the texture of the hair—will hereafter be made the basis of denying to over half the world the right of sharing to their utmost ability the opportunities and privileges of modern civilization.

How shall we conduct ourselves so that in the end human differences will not be emphasized at the expense of human advance?

Goodness and unselfishness; simplicity and honor; tolerance, susceptibility to beauty in form, color and music; courage to look truth in the face; courage to live and suffer in patience and humility, and forgiveness and in hope; eagerness to turn, not simply the other cheek, but the face and the bowed back; capacity to love. In all these mighty things, the greatest things in the world, where do black folk and white folk stand?

What, then, is a race? It is a vast family of human beings, generally of common blood and language, always of common history, traditions and impulses, who are both voluntarily and involuntarily striving together for the accomplishment of certain more or less vividly conceived ideas of life.

Suppose the slaves of 1860 had been white folk.

There is good stock in all races and the outcropping of bad individuals, too.

Some people, to be sure, dream of a future white world. A

glance at any map or newspaper will prove that this is, to say the least, highly improbable.

Think of what has been done in the name of white supremacy right here in the United States.

All men, black and brown, and white, are brothers, varying, through Time and Opportunity, in form and gift and feature, but differing in no essential particular, and alike in soul and in the possibility of infinite development.

Segregation of any set of human beings, be they black, white, or of any color or race is a bad thing, since human contact is the thing that makes for civilization, and human contact is a thing for which all of us are striving to-day.

Racial slander must go. Racial prejudice will follow. Steadfast faith in humanity must come.

The greatest and most immediate danger of white culture, perhaps least sensed, is its fear of the Truth.

What shall this poor world gain if it exchange one race supremacy for another?

The white man, as well as the Negro, is bound and barred by the color-line, and many a scheme of friendliness and philanthropy, of broad-minded sympathy and generous fellowship between the two has dropped still-born because some busybody has forced the color-question to the front and brought the tremendous force of unwritten law against the innovators.

The discovery of personal whiteness among the world's

people is a very modern thing,—a nineteenth- and twentieth-century matter, indeed. The ancient world would have laughed at such a distinction.

The masses of men of all races might be the best of men simply imprisoned by poverty and ignorance.

We forget that once French peasants were the "Niggers" of France, and that German princelings once discussed with doubt the brains and humanity of the bauer.

Meantime, comes the Great Depression. It levels all in mighty catastrophe.

Force and fear have hitherto marked the white attitude toward darker races; shall this continue or be replaced by Freedom and Friendship?

In a world where it means so much to take a man by the hand and sit beside him, look frankly into his eyes and feel his heart beating with red blood; in a world where a social cigar or a cup of tea together means more than legislative halls and magazine articles and speeches,—one can imagine the consequences of the almost utter absence of such social amenities between estranged races.

The opposition to segregation is an opposition to discrimination. The experience in the United States has been that usually when there is racial segregation, there is also racial discrimination.

The attacks that white people themselves have made upon their own moral structure are worse for civilization than anything that any body of Negroes could ever do.

The number of civilized white people is increasing.

The older idea was that the whites would eventually displace the native races and inherit their lands, but this idea has been rudely shaken in the increase of American Negroes, the experience of the English in Africa, India in the West Indies, and the development of South America.

Segregation is impolitic because it is impossible.

Thank God for all those today, few though their voices be, who have not forgotten the divine brotherhood of all men, white and black, rich and poor, fortunate and unfortunate.

Whenever it seems necessary to deny me any privilege, then I am a Negro, and whenever I do anything that is worth doing, suddenly I become preponderantly white.

The curious, most childish propaganda dominates us, and by which good, earnest, even intelligent men have come by millions to believe almost religiously that white folk are a peculiar and chosen people whose one great accomplishment is civilization and that civilization must be protected from the rest of the world by cheating, stealing, lying, and murder.

The persistence in racial distinction spells disaster sooner or later.

There is not today in human affairs a more subtle and awful enemy of human progress of peace and sympathy than the reaction of war and hatred that lurks in the indefinite thing which we call race prejudice.

There must be friendship and goodwill between employer and employee, between black and white.

It is too late in the history of the world to go back to the idea of absolute racial segregation.

We feel and we know that there are many delicate differences in race psychology, numberless changes that our crude social measurements are not yet able to follow minutely, which explain much of history and social development. . . . These considerations have never adequately explained or excused the triumph of brute force and cunning over weakness and innocence.

The race problem is the other side of the labor problem; and the black man's burden is the white man's burden.

This assumption that of all the hues of God whiteness alone is inherently and obviously better than brownness or tan leads to curious acts.

It was not that the French loved or hated Negroes as such; they simply grew to regard them as men with the possibilities and shortcomings of men, added to an unusual natural personal appearance.

There should never be an opposition to segregation pure and simple unless that segregation does involve discrimination.

There is no scientific proof that modern culture is of Nordic origin or that Nordic brains and physique are of better intrinsic quality than Mediterranean, Indian, Chinese, or Negro.

In fact, the proofs of essential human equality of gift are overwhelming.

The only way to make a race self-protecting in its pride is not to degrade it, disfranchise and insult it.

If there are relations between races they must be based on the knowledge and sympathy that come alone from the long and intimate human contact of individuals.

Everything considered, the title to the universe claimed by White Folk is faulty.

Children have no race prejudice. Race feeling and race repulsion only come because of persistent teaching and because scoundrels can profit by it.

If races cannot live together in peace and happiness in America, they cannot live together in the world.

The price of repressing the world's darker races is shown in a moral retrogression and economic waste.

To the American Negro even more than to the white, is the contact with European culture of inestimable value in giving him a broad view of men and affairs, and enabling him to view the problems of his race in their true perspective.

The segregation of human beings purely on a basis of race and color, is not only stupid and unjust, but positively dangerous, since it is a path that leads straight to national jealousies, racial antagonisms, and war.

Neither Roman nor Arab, Greek nor Egyptian, Persian nor Mongol ever took himself and his own perfectness with such disconcerting seriousness as the modern white man. We whose shame, humiliation, and deep insult his aggrandizement so often involved were never deceived.

The assumptions of the anti-segregation campaign have been all wrong. This is not our fault, but it is our misfortune.

We may no longer dodge or hesitate. We must all, black or white, Northerner or Southerner, stand in the light and speak plain words.

If the white, black, brown, and yellow people of the world cannot get along together then the world is doomed.

If it is acknowledged to be unjust to disfranchise a sex it cannot be denied that it is absurd to disfranchise a color.

Europe has never produced and never will in our day bring forth a single human soul who cannot be matched and over-matched in every line of human endeavor by Asia and Africa.

Blood and physical descent are little and idle things as compared with spiritual heritage.

If you were born today a man of some education and knowledge, but born a Japanese or Chinaman, an East Indian or a Negro, what would you do and think?

He [the African American] would not Africanize America, for America has too much to teach the world and Africa. He would not bleach his Negro Soul in a flood of white Americanism, for he knows that Negro blood has a message for the world.

The segregation based mainly and specifically on race and color which the United States Government carries on is despicable, illogical, and uncivilized.

Minority must always vaunt its powers, otherwise, it will lose what little power it has.

Let not color or race be a feature of distinction between white and black men, regardless of worth or ability.

The magic of the word "white" is already broken, and the Color Line in civilization has been crossed in modern times as it was in the great past.

The number of white individuals who are practicing with even reasonable approximation the democracy and unselfishness of Jesus Christ is so small and unimportant as to be fit subject for jest in Sunday supplements.

A physical living together of differing groups and kinds of individuals is possible today to a degree which was unthinkable one, two, and three centuries ago.

The abolition of the lines of vertical race distinction and their tearing away involves fewer chances of degradation and greater opportunities of human betterment than in the case of class lines.

Most men in this world are colored. A faith in humanity, therefore, a belief in the gradual growth and perfectability of men must, if honest, be primarily a belief in colored men.

The problems the world inherits hold the same fatal seed;

world dissention and catastrophe still lurk in the unsolved problems of race relations.

So long as there are artificially emphasized differences of nationality, race and color, not to mention the fundamental discriminations of economic class, there will be no real Humanity.

Is not the world wide enough for two colors, for many little shinings of the sun?

Only faith in humanity will lead the world to rise above its present color prejudice.

This is, or at least we thought it was, the day of the Internation, of Humanity, and the disappearance of race from our vocabulary.

9

Slavery, Lynching, and the Civil War

Although Du Bois escaped being born into slavery by only three years, he grew and lived most of his adult life under the system of American apartheid, not very far removed from that which was abolished in South Africa with the election of Nelson Mandela to that country's presidency in 1994. Referred to in the United States as "Jim Crow segregation," apartheid took many forms—all of which Du Bois addressed in editorials, books, and speeches—at different times and places in the country.

The story of American slavery, from its inception in 1619 to its conclusion with the Civil War in 1865 and the years of reconstruction that followed, was one that Du Bois believed white historians were prone to leave unfinished. The epic struggle between the North and South over the continuation of slavery was only part of what defined its history. Enslavement itself was tragic enough, but possibly hundreds of millions had been either killed or died at various stages of capture and transportation: in the bush and on the shores of Africa itself, during the horrific Middle Passage, and following arrival to the United States. At the root of slavery and its ultimate demise were issues of economics, a demand for labor to further the growth of a young country, and industrial advancement. These in turn developed into moral and political issues that the country sought to resolve by various means, including transporting blacks to Africa, abolishing slavery in the North, and ultimately civil war.

Du Bois did not view American slavery so much with the emotional fury of a black man outraged at the abuse of his people as he did with the cool detachment of a scientist at work. Slavery itself, he often pointed out, was not an American invention. In his groundbreaking works *The Suppression of the African Slave-Trade to the United States of America, 1638–1870*, in 1896, and *Black Reconstruction in America 1860–1880*, in 1935, Du Bois portrayed institutional slavery as the result of a series of economic miscalculations, political missteps, and moral judgment obscured by personal agendas for power and influence. That whites came to equate slavery with blackness was an error that impeded both the liberation of African Americans and the establishment of genuine democracy. It also blinded them to the authentic and valuable contributions of blacks to American culture.

Completing the story of slavery meant acknowledging the many black abolitionists who advocated for the freedom of slaves. It further meant recognition of the thousands of African Americans who fought to free themselves during the Civil War as opposed to waiting for emancipation.

Moreover, the Black Codes adopted by southern legislators when Du Bois was an infant all but re-instated slavery. In some states, blacks were subject to imprisonment if not employed by a white person, or they could be beaten at whim by the same. The increasing practice of murdering African Americans by lynching during this period would not cease for nearly another century. Yet, as Du Bois would point out time and again, the truly miraculous part of the story of slavery and its aftermath was not the cruelties and destruction that blacks continued to suffer: it was the gifts of song, innovation, genius, and leadership they continued to provide in spite of their suffering.

Easily the most dramatic episode in American history was the sudden move to free four million black slaves in an effort to stop a great civil war, to end forty years of great controversy, and to appease the moral sense of civilization.

No one can read that first thin autobiography of Frederick Douglass and have left many illusions about slavery.

John Brown loved his neighbor as himself. He could not endure, therefore, to see his neighbor poor, unfortunate, or oppressed.

The very man who is called the Emancipator declared again and again that his object was the integrity of the Union and not the emancipation of the slaves; that if he could keep the Union from being disrupted, he would not only allow slavery to exist but would loyally protect it.

In proportion to population, more Negroes than whites fought in the Civil War.

By reason of a crime (perhaps the greatest crime in human history) the modern world has been systematically taught to despise colored peoples.

If in the hey-day of the greatest of the world's civilizations, it is possible for one people ruthlessly to steal another, drag them helpless across the water, enslave them, debauch them, and then slowly murder them by economic and social exclusion until they disappear from the face of the earth—if the consumation of such a crime be possible in the twentieth century, then our civilization is vain and the republic is a mockery and a farce.

The North went to war without the slightest idea of freeing the slave. . . . The great majority of Northerners from Lincoln down pledged themselves to protect slavery, and they hated and harried abolitionists.

It is neither profitable nor in accordance with scientific truth to consider that whatever the constitutional fathers did was right, or that slavery was a plague sent from God and fated to be eliminated in due time.

The South believed an educated Negro to be a dangerous Negro. And the South was not wholly wrong.

The South because of slavery has lagged behind the rest of the world. It must catch up.

A nation with a great disease set out to rescue civilization; it took the disease with it in virulent form and that disease of race-hatred and prejudice hampered its actions and discredited its finest professions.

The Civil War was an attempt of white laborers in the United States to get western land and higher wages by confining Negroes to slavery and the South. This meant that the Negro before and after emancipation, in self-defense was propelled toward the employing class and the employing class was quick to take advantage of this.

Lynching [was] a barbarism of a degree of contemptible nastiness unparalleled in human history. Yet for fifty years we have lynched two Negroes a week, and we have kept this up right through the war [World War I].

Lynching in the United States, even the almost incredible

burning of human beings alive, have raised not a ripple of interest, not a single protest from the United States government, scarcely a word from the pulpit and not a syllable of horror or suggestion from the Defenders of the Republic, the 100 percent Americans or the propagandists of the army and navy.

Lynching is a national evil of which Negroes are the chief victims. It is perhaps the greatest disgrace from which this country suffers.

The free Negro leader early arose and his chief characteristic was intense earnestness and deep feeling on the slavery question.

The using of men for the benefit of masters is no new invention of modern Europe. It is quite as old as the world.

The South was ashamed because it fought to perpetuate human slavery. The North was ashamed because it had to call in the black men to save the Union, abolish slavery, and establish democracy.

For two or more centuries America has marched proudly in the van of human hatred—making bonfires of human flesh and laughing at them hideously, and making the insulting of millions more than a matter of dislike—rather a great religion, a world war-cry.

Until, then, colored people have a voice in the community, surrender to the domination of the white South is unthinkable.

Every experiment of such a kind, however, where the moral

standard of a people is lowered for the sake of a material advantage, is dangerous in just such proportion as that advantage is great.

The colonists themselves declared slaves the strength and sinews of this western world, and the lack of them "the grand obstruction" here, as the settlements "cannot subsist without supplies of them."

Three things American slavery gave the Negro—the habit of work, the English language, and the Christian religion; but one priceless thing it debauched, destroyed, and took from him, and that was the organized home.

The history of slavery and the slave-trade after 1820 must be read in the light of the industrial revolution through which the civilized world passed in the first half of the nineteenth century.

To say that a nation is in the way of civilization is a contradiction in terms, and a system of human culture whose principles is the rise of one race on the ruins of another is a farce and a lie.

Modern African slavery was the beginning of the modern labor problem, and must be looked at and interpreted from that point of view unless we would lose ourselves in an altogether false analogy. Modern world commerce, modern imperialism, the modern factory system, and the modern labor problem began with the African slave trade.

The Klan is at once criminal and victim.

The white community, undoubtedly, wants to keep the Negro

in the country as a peasant under working conditions least removed from slavery.

The mob often does vicariously that which the aristocrats want done but do not soil their hands with.

Abolitionists attacked slavery because it was wrong and their moral battle cannot be truthfully minimized or forgotten.

If truth is our object, no amount of flowery romance and the personal reminiscences of its protected beneficiaries can keep the world from knowing that slavery was a cruel, dirty, costly, and inexcusable anachronism, which nearly ruined the world's greatest experiment in democracy.

The main differences in motive between the restrictions which the planting and the farming colonies put on the African slave-trade, lay in the fact that the former limited it mainly from fear of insurrection, the latter mainly because it did not pay.

Ever have men striven to conceive of their victims as different from the victors, endlessly different, in soul and blood, strength and cunning, race and lineage.

The Southern planters, born and reared in a slave system, thought that someday the system might change, and possibly disappear; but active effort to this end on their part was ever farthest from their thoughts. Here, then, began that fatal policy toward slavery and the slave-trade that characterized the nation for three-quarters of a century, the policy of laissez-faire, laissez-passer.

The vision of "forty acres and a mule"—the righteous and

reasonable ambition to become a land holder, which the nation had all but categorically promised the freedmen—was destined in most cases to bitter disappointment.

Had the country been conceived of as existing primarily for the benefit of its actual inhabitants, it might have waited for natural increase or immigration to supply the needed hands; but both Europe and the earlier colonists themselves regarded this land as existing chiefly for the benefit of Europe, and as designed to be exploited, as rapidly and ruthlessly as possible, of the boundless wealth of its resources. This was the primary excuse for the rise of the African slave-trade to America.

Like all primitive folk, the slave stood near to Nature's heart.

Endowed with a rich topical imagination and a keen, delicate appreciation of Nature, the transplanted African lived in a world animate with gods and devils, elves and witches; full of strange influences—of Good to be implored, of evil to be propitiated. Slavery, then, was to him the dark triumph of Evil over him.

Of death the Negro showed little fear, but talked of it familiarly and even fondly as simply a crossing of the waters, perhaps—who knows?—back to his ancient forests again.

The clique of political philosophers to which Jefferson belonged never imagined the continued existence of the country with slavery.

A third party in the United Sates is impossible on account of the Solid South. They are a dead weight and handicap to all political reform. They have but one shibboleth and that is the Negro.

The exact proportions of the slave-trade to America can be but approximately determined.

Even in the matter of enforcing its own laws and co-operating with the civilized world, a lethargy seized the country, and it did not awake until slavery was about to destroy it.

It was only a peculiar and almost fortuitous commingling of moral, political, and economic motives that eventually crushed African slavery and its handmaid, the slave-trade in America.

It behooves the United States, therefore, in the interest both of scientific truth and future social reform, carefully to study such chapters of the history as that of the suppression of the slave-trade.

Men came to the idea of exclusive black slavery by gradually enslaving the workers, as was the world's long custom, and then gradually conceiving certain sorts of work and certain colors of men as necessarily connected.

The freedmen, far from being the inert recipients of freedom at the hands of philanthropists, furnished 200,000 soldiers in the Civil War who took part in nearly 200 battles and skirmishes, and in addition perhaps 300,000 others as effective laborers and helpers.

A nation cannot exist half slave and half free. Either the slave will rise through blood or the freeman will sink.

I shall forgive the white South much in its final judgment day: I shall forgive its slavery, for slavery is a world-old habit; I shall forgive its fighting for a well-lost cause, and for remembering that struggle with tender tears; I shall forgive its so-called "pride of race," the passion of its hot blood, and even its dear, old, laughable strutting and posing; but one thing I shall never forgive, neither in this world nor the world to come: its wanton and continued and persistent insulting of the black womanhood which it sought and seeks to prostitute to its lust.

The Negro slave trade was the first step in modern world commerce, followed by the modern theory of colonial expansion. Slaves as an article of commerce were shipped as long as the traffic paid.

The transition period between slavery and freedom is a dangerous and critical one.

Of all human development, ancient and modern, not the least singular and significant is the philosophy of life and action which slavery bred in the souls of black folk.

A printer and a carpenter, a rail-splitter and a tailor— Garrison, Christ, Lincoln, and Johnson, were the tools of the greatest moral awakening America ever knew, chosen to challenge capital invested in the bodies of men and annul the private profit of slavery.

What did it mean to be a slave? It is hard to imagine it today. We think of oppression beyond all conception: cruelty, degradation, whipping, and starvation, the absolute negation of human rights; or on the contrary, we may think of the ordinary worker the world over today, slaving ten, twelve, or fourteen hours a day, without enough to eat, compelled by his physical necessities to do this and not to do that, curtailed in his movements and his possibilities; and we say, here, too, is a slave called a "free worker," and slavery is merely a matter of name.... But there was in 1863 a real meaning to slavery different from that we may apply to the laborer today. It was in part psychological, the enforced personal feeling of inferiority, the calling of another Master; the standing with hat in hand. It was the helplessness.

To most of the four million black folk emancipated by civil war, God was real. They knew Him. They had met Him personally in many a wild orgy of religious frenzy, or in the black stillness of the night. His plan for them was clear; they were to suffer and be degraded, and then afterwards by Divine edict, raised to manhood and power; and so on January 1, 1863, He made them free.

The espousal of the doctrine of Negro inferiority by the South was primarily because of economic motives and the inter-connected political urge necessary to support slave industry; but to the watching world it sounded like the carefully thought out result of experience and reason; and because of this it was singularly disastrous for modern civilization in science and religion, in art and government, as well as in industry.

The Southerners were as little conscious of the hurt they were inflicting on human beings as the Northerners were of their treatment of the insane.

Suddenly, there was Reason in all this mad orgy. Suddenly the world knew why this blundering horror of civil war had to be. God had come to America, and the land, fire-drunk, howled the hymn of joy.

There came the slow looming of emancipation. Crowds and armies of the unknown, inscrutable, unfathomable Yankees: cruelty behind and before; rumors of a new slave trade; but slowly, continuously, the wild truth, the bitter truth, the magic truth, came surging through.

Sexual chaos was always the possibility of slavery, not always realized but always possible.

Southerners who had suckled food from black breasts vied with each other in fornication with black women, and even in beastly incest. They took the name of their fathers in vain to seduce their own sisters.

The abolition of slavery meant not simply abolition of legal ownership of the slave; it meant the uplift of slaves and their eventual incorporation into the body civil, politic, and social, of the United States. There was, of course, much difference as to the exact extent of this incorporation, but less and less desire to limit it in any way by law.

There were the free Negroes: those of the North free in some cases for many generations, and voters; and in other cases, fugitives, new come from the South, with little skill and small knowledge of life and labor in their new environment. There were the free Negroes of the South, an unstable, harried class, living on sufferance of the law, and the good will of white patrons, and yet rising to be workers and sometimes owners of property and even of slaves, and cultured citizens. There was the great mass of poor whites, disinherited of their economic portion by competition with the slave system, and land monopoly.

Fugitive slaves, like Frederick Douglass and others humbler and less gifted, increased the number of abolitionists by thousands and spelled the doom of slavery.

The slavery of Negroes in the South was not usually a deliberately cruel and oppressive system. It did not mean systematic starvation or murder. On the other hand, it is just as difficult to conceive as quite true the idyllic picture of a patriarchal state with cultured and humane masters under whom slaves were as children, guided and trained in work and play, given even such mental training as was for their good, and for the well-being of the surrounding world.

The hurt to the Negro in this era was not only his treatment in slavery; it was the wound dealt to his reputation as a human being.

The inevitable result of the Civil War eventually had to be the enfranchisement of the laboring class, black and white, in the South. It could not, as the South clamored to make it, result in the mere legalistic freeing of the slaves.

The Southern planter suffered, not simply for his economic mistakes—the psychological effect of slavery upon him was fatal. The mere fact that man could be, under the law, the actual master of the mind and body of human beings had to have disastrous effects. It tended to inflate the ego of most planters beyond all reason; they became arrogant, strutting, quarrelsome kinglets; they issued commands; they made laws; they shouted their orders; they expected deference and self-abasement; they were choleric and easily insulted. Their "honor" became a vast and awful thing, requiring wide and insistent deference. Such of them as were inherently weak and inefficient were all the more easily angered, jealous and resentful; while the few who were superior, physically or mentally, conceived no bounds to their power and personal prestige. As the world had long learned, nothing is so calculated to ruin human nature as absolute power over human beings.

So long as slavery was a matter of race and color, it made the conscience of the nation uneasy and continually affronted its ideals. The men who wrote the Constitution sought by every evasion, and almost by subterfuge, to keep recognition of slavery out of the basic form of the new government. They founded their hopes on the prohibition of the slave trade, being sure that without continual additions from abroad, this tropical people would not long survive, and thus the problem of slavery would disappear in death. They miscalculated, or did not foresee the changing economic world.

From all that has been written and said about the ante-bellum South, one almost loses sight of about 5,000,000 white people in 1860 who lived in the South and held no slaves. Even among the two million slaveholders, an oligarchy of 8,000 really ruled the South.

With all its fine men and sacrificing women, its hospitable homes and graceful manners, the South turned the most beautiful section of the nation into a center of poverty and suffering, of drinking, gambling and brawling; an abode of ignorance among black and white more abysmal than in

any modern land; and a system of industry so humanly unjust and economically inefficient that if it had not committed suicide in civil war, it would have disintegrated of its
own weight.

Even those who saw the seamy side of slavery were convinced of the rightness of the system because they believed
that there were seeds of disaster in the North against which
slavery would be their protection.

Into the hands of the slaveholders the political power of the
South was concentrated, by their social prestige, by property ownership and also by the extraordinary rule of the
counting of all or at least three-fifths of the Negroes as part
of the basis of presentation in the legislature.

The persons who were buying slaves in the cotton belt were
not buying families, they were buying workers, and thus by
economic demand families were continually and regularly
broken up; the father was sold away; the mother and the
half-grown children separated, and sometimes smaller children were sold. One of the subsequent tragedies of the system was the frantic efforts, before and after emancipation,
of Negroes hunting for their relatives throughout the United
States.

The giant forces of water and of steam were harnessed to do
the world's work, and the black workers of America bent at
the bottom of a growing pyramid of commerce and industry; and they not only could not be spared, if this new economic organization was to expand, but rather they became
the cause of new political demands and alignments, or new
dreams of power and visions of empire.

Nothing else of art or religion did the slave South give to the world, except the Negro song and story. And even after slavery, down to our day, it has added but little to this gift.

The only curb upon the power of the master was his sense of humanity and decency, on the one hand, and the conserving of his investment on the other.

Human slavery in the South pointed and led in two singularly contradictory and paradoxical directions—toward the deliberate commercial breeding and sale of human labor for profit and toward the intermingling of black and white blood. The slaveholders shrank from acknowledging either set of facts but they were clear and undeniable.

Slavery bred in the poor white a dislike of Negro toil of all sorts. He never regarded himself as a laborer, or as part of any labor movement. If he had any ambition at all it was to become a planter and to own "niggers." To these Negroes he transferred all the dislike and hatred which he had for the whole slave system. The result was that the system was held stable and intact by the poor white.

Slaves were not considered men. They had no right of petition. They were "devisable like any other chattel." They could own nothing; they could make no contracts; they could hold no property, nor traffic in property; they could not hire out; they could not legally marry nor constitute families; they could not control their children; they could not appeal from their master; they could be punished at will. They could not testify in court; they could be imprisoned by their owners, and the criminal offense of assault and battery could not be committed on the person of a slave.

The system [of slavery] often so affronted the moral sense of the planters themselves that they tried to hide from it. They could not face the fact of Negro women as brood mares and of black children as puppies.

10

AFRICA

Much of the widespread colonization of Africa that would command so much of Du Bois's political attention as an adult took place while he was a child. In adulthood, he would often refer to the colonization of the continent as a form of "rape" and indicate a parallel between the political abuse of Africa the continent and the moral and physical abuse of those Africans who became slaves in the United States.

During his days as editor of *Crisis* magazine and board member of the National Association for the Advancement of Colored People, he rejected for African Americans the notion of a "return to Africa" as was once fostered by such stalwarts as *North Star* co-editor Martin Robison Delany, Georgia State representative Bishop Henry McNeal Turner, and Du Bois's one-time mentor, the priest and educator Alexander Crummell. Rather than the promise of political refuge—as indeed it would become for him in his last year— what Africa had to offer humanity was not a dead end of regrets over the past but an open road of possibilities for the future. Essential, however, to traveling that open road of endless possibility was an acknowledgment of the continent's great place in history as something much more than Europe's concubine, but rather as the matriarch of every civilization that ever did or would exist.

Whereas the events of history could not be altered, the world's knowledge of it in regard to Africa could and should be expanded. It had been and yet remained much more than a found treasure plundered by Europeans. Whether her gifts were those of such material wealth as gold, ivory, and dia-

monds, or of such intellectual wealth as the spiritual philosophies of Egypt, the agricultural science of Sierra Leone,
and the craftsmanship of Ghana and Nigeria, Du Bois noted
that Africa was always "giving us something new or some
metempsychosis of a world-old thing." Always. Such gen-
erosity of spirit and purse and self did not deserve to be
ridiculed or abused in any manner. It deserved to be honored.

Yonder behind the horizon is Cape Bojadur whence in 1441
came the brown Moors and black Moors who through the
slave trade built America and modern commerce and let
loose the furies of the world.

My ship seeks Africa.

The father and his worship is Asia; Europe is the precon-
scious, self-centered, forward-striving child; but the land of
the mother is and was Africa.

Nearly every human empire that has arisen in the world,
material and spiritual, has found some of its greatest crises
on this continent of Africa, from Greece to Great Britain.

The most magnificent drama in the last thousand years of
human history is the transportation of ten million human
beings out of the dark beauty of their mother continent into
the new-found Eldorado of the West.

Through the slave trade Africa lost at least 100,000,000
human beings, with all the attendant misery and economic
and social disorganization.

Lying treaties, rivers of rum, murder, assassination, mutilation, rape, and torture have marked the progress of Englishman, German, Frenchman, and Belgian on the Dark Continent. The only way in which the world has been able to endure the horrible tale is by deliberately stopping its ear and changing the subject of conversation while the devilry went on.

African migration [for African Americans] is a century-old and pretty thoroughly discredited dream.

All over Africa has gone this shameless monopolizing of land and natural resources to force poverty on the masses and reduce them to the "dumb-driven-cattle" stage of labor activity.

Always Africa is giving us something new or some metempsychosis of a world-old thing.

The indictment of Africa against Europe is grave.

If, by reason of carelessness, prejudice, greed, and injustice, the black world is to be exploited and vanished and degraded, the results must be deplorable, if not fatal—not simply to them, but to the high ideals of justice, freedom, and culture which a thousand years of Christian civilization have held before Europe.

Egypt too is Africa.

Reverence for humanity, as such, must be installed in the world, and Africa should be the talisman.

The subtle folk-lore of Africa, with whimsy and parable, veiled wish and wisdom.

Not only then in the [eighteen] forties and fifties did the word "Negro" lose its capital letter, but African history became the tale of degraded animals and sub-human savages, where no vestige of human culture found foothold.

11

History and the World

The first half of the twentieth century in the United States and much of the world was an era when racial and ethnic differences determined even the most uncontrived actions. Stepping into a restaurant, boarding a train, engaging in sexual relationships, or running or voting for a public office were all ruled by notions of differences between groups. Race remained an element that tempted society in general and historians in particular to half-truths, shortsightedness, and outright falsifications. However, as Du Bois noted in his many observations on the nature of history, it was important to realize that the record of human interaction was much more than an account of entanglements between people with varying shades of skin color. It was also the log of humankind's ability or inability to rise above age-old phobias, the persistent pain of ignorance, and the perennial disgrace of perennial war.

Men and women recognizing history for the master teacher that it was, would do well to sit at its feet and absorb the many valuable lessons it had to share, no matter how hurtful or embarrassing some might be. Historians who willfully employed history (and one could easily add religion to or substitute it for this equation) to magnify the achievements of one group while diluting those of another, undermined history's potential "to guide the world nearer and nearer that perfection of human life for which we all long." By adhering to the details of "the things that actually happened in the world," it becomes apparent enough that glorious achievements and dismal failures filled entire chapters in every group's story.

A sincere respect for the integrity of historical truth also made it possible to acknowledge that the domination of one group by another—be the division by race or gender or class or religion—was not the only possibility for nations in the twentieth century. That such domination had occurred in history was irrefutable. However, equally irrefutable were instances of cooperation between different social groups and those moments of invention and advancement not characterized at all by group interaction but born of the labors of individuals within groups. Women had been leaders as well as followers. Blacks had been world travelers and heads of kingdoms as well as slaves. Europeans and Asians had engaged in peaceful trade as well as ruinous war. In short, the greatest lesson from the master teacher history was very possibly an expanded awareness of the options for human interaction available to the world. The startling gift of modern life was the ability to choose from an array of possibilities with an informed intelligence and thus extend the record of humanity's glory rather than glorify the record of its infamy and annihilation.

You must not make the mistake of misunderstanding the age in which you live.

What we have got to know, so far as possible, are the things that actually happened in the world.

When in the world's history struggling human beings have in doubt and travail, in weariness and anxiety, established a great engine of human betterment, it behooves us to sit and see and hope in God's good time to help—to ask what they did and how they did it and who were the men that did these things.

The historian has no right posing as scientist, to conceal or distort facts.

In human history the improbable has often happened.

If history is going to be scientific; if the record of human actions is going to be set down with that accuracy and faithfulness of detail which will allow its use as a measuring rod and guidepost for the future of nations, there must be set some standards of ethics in research and interpretations.

History plays curious tricks.

The English nation stood for constitutional liberty and commercial freedom; the German nation for science and philosophy; the Romance nations stood for literature and art, and the other race groups are striving, each in its own way to develop for civilization its particular message, its particular ideal, which shall help to guide the world nearer and nearer that perfection of human life for which we all long, that "one far off Divine event."

The nineteenth was the first century of human sympathy,— the age when half wonderingly we began to descry in others that transfigured spark of divinity which we call Myself.

One is astonished in the study of history at the recurrence of the idea that evil must be forgotten, distorted, skimmed over.

The Negro blood which flowed in the veins of many of the

mightiest of the Pharoahs, accounts for much of Egyptian art, and indeed, Egyptian civilization owes much in its origins to the development of the large strains of Negro blood which manifested itself in every grade of Egyptian society.

We see Europe's greatest sin precisely where we found Africa's and Asia's—in human hatred.

Little of beauty has America given the world save the rude grandeur God himself stamped on her bosom; the human spirit in this new world has expressed itself in vigor and ingenuity rather than in beauty.

The Anglo-Saxon love a soldier—Jefferson Davis was an Anglo-Saxon, Jefferson Davis was a soldier.

History is economic history; living is earning a living.

Why, then, is Europe great? Because of the foundations which the mighty past have furnished her to build upon: the iron trade of ancient, black Africa, the religion and empire-building of yellow Asia, the art and science of the "dago" Mediterranean shore, east, south, and west, as well as north.

Liberia and Haiti were never given a sincere chance and were from first to last harassed, as only modern capitalism can harass little and hated nations.

We founded a republic in 1787 which was in reality an aristocracy of the most pronounced tendencies.

The treatment of the period of Reconstruction reflects small credit upon American historians as scientists. We have too often a deliberate attempt so to change the facts of history that the story will make pleasant reading for Americans.

The extraordinary history of the rise and triumph of the poor whites has been largely neglected, even by Southern white students.

We shall never have a science of history until we have in our colleges men who regard the truth as more important than the defense of the white race.

In propaganda against the Negro since emancipation in this land, we face one of the most stupendous efforts the world ever saw to discredit human beings, an effort involving universities, history, science, social life, and religion.

In ancient Mediterranean civilization Negro blood was predominant in many great nations and present in nearly all.

Admitting that in the world's history again and again that this or that race has outstripped another in culture, it is impossible to prove that inherent racial superiority was the cause or that the level of culture has been permanently raised in one race by keeping other races down.

The growing exploitation of white labor in Europe, the rise of the factory system, the increased monopoly of land, and the problem of the distribution of political power, began to send wave after wave of immigrants to America, looking for new freedom, new opportunity, and new democracy.

12

Poetry, Prayers, and Parables

In an essay titled "Of Alexander Crummell," included in his 1903 masterpiece *The Souls of Black Folk*, Du Bois penned "the history of a human heart," and the triumph of an exceptional man who struggled throughout his adult life against the "temptations" of hatred, despair, doubt, and humiliation. The portrait Du Bois paints in this eulogy of the educator, priest, and Pan-Africanist Crummell is one of a spiritual servant within an increasingly material world, who embraced with faith, courage, intelligence, and love, the challenges of a unique and demanding life at an equally unique and demanding period in history. His observations of "the sweetness of his strength," his prophetic sensibility, and nearly saint-like bearing were qualities that many came to apply to Du Bois himself, despite the strength of character and self-assurance that some interpreted as arrogance.

Du Bois's chosen purposes for his life, like those chosen by the priest Crummell for his, included a desire to assist with the further development of human civilization on as many levels as possible, and to do that largely by helping to elevate the social, economic, and political status of oppressed peoples all over the world, particularly those of African descent. Brotherhood and sisterhood across lines of color, culture, and class was not so much something men needed to create as it was something they simply failed to accept.

In his calls for social justice, racial equity, economic parity, and worldwide peace, Du Bois perhaps engaged as much in dialogue with his God as with his fellow man. That people of different races and cultures had much to share with one another while electing instead to ostracize each other could be viewed as something of a divine mystery. That individuals so often apparently chose the chaos of barbarity over the harmony of civility, the destructiveness of hatred over the constructiveness of love, and the blindness of violence over the clear intelligence of peace, could be taken as a cosmic farce. If this were so, then all debates to the existence or non-existence of God aside, the cure for the world's fatal ills was not in the hands of human beings.

Living his life as a public servant dedicated to bridging the many gaps that divided humankind from humankind meant many sacrifices on behalf of Du Bois. Constant travel to conferences, organizational meetings, and to deliver speeches and lectures required time away from his beloved family. Taking public stands meant taking visible risks and, when in error, suffering public embarrassment. Such was the case when he endorsed Woodrow Wilson's presidential campaign only to later regret it bitterly when Wilson ordered the racial segregation of public facilities in Washington, D.C. And employment with the National Association for the Advancement of Colored People—neither impoverishing him nor making him wealthy—meant foregoing the kind of affluence he might have attained, holding the first Ph.D awarded to an African American by Harvard University, by pursuing the position of a university department head or presidency as did his fellow sociologist and Harlem Renaissance participant, Charles Spurgeon Johnson.

In his political speeches and historical writings, Du Bois fought his ideological battles. In the kinds of poems and parables like those that follow, he often prayed. Sometimes, like the psalmist David, his prayers were for divine vengeance, sometimes for truth, or understanding, or faith and strength and the will to endure. Very possibly it was his hope that one day someone might have reason to say of him what he imagined at the end of his essay on Crummell that Christ must have said upon greeting the priest's weary spirit: "Well done!"

Credo

I believe in God who made of one blood all races that dwell on earth. I believe that all men, black and brown and white, are brothers, varying through Time and Opportunity, in form and gift and feature, but differing in no essential particular, and alike in soul and in the possibility of infinite development.

Especially do I believe in the Negro Race; in the beauty of its genius, the sweetness of its soul and its strength in that meekness which shall yet inherit this turbulent earth.

I believe in pride of race and lineage and self; in pride of self so deep as to scorn injustice to other selves; in pride of lineage so great as to despise no man's father; in pride of race so chivalrous as neither to offer bastardry to the weak nor beg wedlock of the strong, knowing that men may be brothers in Christ, even they be not brothers-in-law.

I believe in Service—humble reverent service, from the blackening of boots to the whitening of souls; for Work is Heaven, Idleness hell, and Wage is the "Well Done!" of the master who summoned all them that labor and are heavy laden, making no distinction between the black sweating cotton-hands of Georgia and the First Families of Virginia, since all distinction not based on deed is devilish and not divine.

I believe in the Devil and his angels, who wantonly work to narrow the opportunity of struggling human beings, especially if they be black; who spit in the faces of the fallen, strike them that cannot strike again, believe the worst and work to prove it, hating the image which their Maker stamped on a brother's soul.

I believe in the Prince of Peace. I believe that War is Murder. I believe that armies and navies are at bottom the tinsel and braggadocio of oppression and wrong; and I believe that the wicked conquest of weaker and darker nations by nations whiter and stronger but foreshadows the death of that strength.

I believe in Liberty for all men; the space to stretch their arms and their souls; the right to breathe and the right to vote, the freedom to choose their friends, enjoy the sunshine and ride on the railroads, uncursed by color; thinking, dreaming, working as they will in a kingdom of God and love.

I believe in the training of children, black even as white; the leading out of little souls into the green pastures and beside the still waters, not for self or peace, but for Life lit by some large vision of beauty and goodness and truth; lest we forget, and the sons of the fathers, like Esau, for more meat barter their birthright in a mighty nation.

Finally, I believe in Patience—patience with the weakness of the Weak and the strength of the Strong, the prejudice of the ignorant and the ignorance of the Blind; patience with the tardy triumph of Joy and the mad chastening of Sorrow—patience with God.

Jesus Christ in Texas

It was in Waco, Texas.

The convict guard laughed. "I don't know," he said, "I hadn't thought of that." He hesitated and looked at the stranger curiously. In the solemn twilight he got an impression of unusual height and soft, dark eyes. "Curious sort of acquaintance for the colonel," he thought; then he continued aloud: "But that nigger there is bad, a born thief, and ought to be sent up for life; got ten years last time—"

Here the voice of the promoter, talking within, broke in; he was bending over his figures, sitting by the colonel. He was slight, with a sharp nose.

"The convicts," he said, " would cost us $96 a year and board. Well, we can squeeze this so that it won't be over $125 apiece. Now if these fellows are driven, they can build this line within twelve months. It will be running by next April. Freights will fall fifty per cent. Why, man, you'll be a millionaire in less than ten years."

The colonel started. He was a thick, short man, with a clean-shaven face and a certain air of breeding about the lines of his countenance; the word "millionaire" sounded well to his ears. He thought—he thought a great deal; he almost heard the puff of the fearfully costly automobile that was coming up the road, and he said:

"I suppose we might as well hire them."

"Of course," answered the promoter.

The voice of the tall stranger in the corner broke in here:

"It will be a good thing for them?" he said, half in question.

The colonel moved. "The guard makes strange friends," he thought to himself. "What's this man doing here, anyway?" He looked at him, or rather looked at his eyes, and then somehow he felt a warming toward him. He said:

"Well, at least, it can't harm them; they're beyond that."

"It will do them good, then," said the stranger again.

The promoter shrugged his shoulders. "It will do us good," he said.

But the colonel shook his head impatiently. He felt a desire to justify himself before those eyes, and he answered: "Yes, it will do them good; or at any rate it won't make them any worse than they are." Then he started to say something else, but here sure enough the sound of the automobile breathing at the gate stopped him and they all arose.

"It is settled, then," said the promoter.

"Yes," said the colonel, turning toward the stranger again. "Are you going into town?" he asked with the Southern courtesy of white men to white men in a country town. The stranger said he was. "Then come along in my machine. I want to talk with you about this."

They went out to the car. The stranger as he went turned again to look back at the convict. He was a tall, powerfully built black fellow. His face was sullen, with a low forehead, thick, hanging lips, and bitter eyes. There was revolt written about his mouth despite the hang-dog expression. He stood bending over his pile of stones, pounding listlessly. Beside him stood a boy of twelve—yellow, with a hunted, crafty look. The convict raised his eyes and they met the eyes of the stranger. The hammer fell from his hands.

The stranger turned slowly toward the automobile and the colonel introduced him. He had not exactly caught his name, but he mumbled something as he presented him to his wife and little girl, who were waiting.

As they whirled away the colonel started to talk, but the stranger had taken the little girl into his lap and together they conversed in low tones all the way home.

In some way, they did not exactly know how, they got the impression that the man was a teacher and, of course, he must be a foreigner. The long, cloak-like coat told this. They rode in the twilight through the lighted town and at last drew up before the colonel's mansion, with its ghost-like pillars.

The lady in the back seat was thinking of the guests she had invited to dinner and was wondering if she ought not to ask this man to stay. He seemed cultured and she supposed he was some acquaintance of the colonel's. It would be rather interesting to have him there, with the judge's wife and daughter and the rector. She spoke, almost before she thought:

"You will enter and rest awhile?"

The colonel and the little girl insisted. For a moment the stranger seemed about to refuse. He said he had some business for his father, about town. Then for the child's sake he consented.

Up the steps they went and into the dark parlor where they sat and talked a long time. It was a curious conversation. Afterwards they did not remember exactly what was said and yet they all remembered a certain strange satisfaction in that long, low talk.

Finally the nurse came for the reluctant child and the hostess bethought herself:

"We will have a cup of tea; you will be dry and tired."

She rang and switched on a blaze of light. With one accord they all looked at the stranger, for they had hardly seen him well in the glooming twilight. The woman started in amazement and the colonel half rose in anger. Why, the man was a mulatto, surely; even if he did not own the Negro blood, their practiced eyes knew it. He was tall and straight and the coat looked like a Jewish gabardine. His hair hung in close curls far down the sides of his face and his face was olive, even yellow.

A peremptory order rose to the colonel's lips and froze there as he caught the stranger's eyes. Those eyes—where had he seen those eyes before? He remembered them long years ago. The soft, tear-filled eyes of a brown girl. He remembered many things, and his face grew drawn and white. Those eyes kept burning into him, even when they were turned half away toward the staircase, where the white figure of the child hovered with her nurse and waved good-night. The lady sank into her chair and thought: "What will the judge's wife say? How did the colonel come to invite this man here? How shall we be rid of him?" She looked at the colonel in reproachful consternation.

Just then the door opened and the old butler came in. He was an ancient black man, with tufted white hair, and he held before him a large, silver tray filled with a china tea service. The stranger rose slowly and stretched forth his hands as if to bless the viands. The old man paused in bewilderment, tottered, and then with sudden gladness in his eyes dropped to his knees, and the tray crashed to the floor.

"My Lord and my God!" he whispered; but the woman screamed: "Mother's china!"

The doorbell rang.

"Heavens! Here is the dinner party!" exclaimed the lady. She turned toward the door, but there in the hall, clad in her night clothes, was the little girl. She had stolen down the stairs to see the stranger again, and the nurse above was calling in vain. The woman felt hysterical and scolded at the nurse, but the stranger had stretched out his arms and with a glad cry the child nestled in them. They caught some words about the "Kingdom of Heaven" as he slowly mounted the stairs with his little, white burden.

The mother was glad of anything to get rid of the interloper, even for a moment. The bell rang again and she hastened toward the door, which the loitering black maid was just opening. She did not notice the shadow of the stranger as he came slowly down the stairs and paused by the newel post, dark and silent.

The judge's wife came in. She was an old woman, frilled and powdered into a semblance of youth, and gorgeously gowned. She came forward, smiling with extended hands, but when she was opposite the stranger, somewhere a chill seemed to strike her and she shuddered and cried:

"What a draft!" as she drew a silken shawl about her and shook hands cordially; she forgot to ask who the stranger was. The judge strode in unseeing, thinking of a puzzling case of theft.

"Eh? What? Oh—er—yes,—good evening," he said, "good evening." Behind them came a young woman in the glory of youth, and daintily silked, beautiful in face and form, with diamonds around her fair neck. She came in lightly, but stopped with a little gasp; then she laughed gaily and said:

"Why, I beg your pardon. Was it not curious? I thought I saw there behind your man"—she hesitated, but he must be a servant, she argued—"the shadow of great, white wings. It was but the light on the drapery. What a turn it gave me." And she smiled again. With her came a tall, handsome, young naval officer. Hearing his lady refer to the servant, he hardly looked at him, but held his gilded cap carelessly toward him, and the stranger placed it carefully on the rack.

Last came the rector, a man of forty, and well clothed. He started to pass the stranger, stopped, and looked at him inquiringly.

"I beg your pardon," he said. "I beg your pardon—I think I have met you?"

The stranger made no answer, and the hostess nervously hurried the guests on. But the rector lingered and looked perplexed.

"Surely, I know you. I have met you somewhere," he said, putting his hand vaguely to his head. "You remember me, do you not?"

The stranger quietly swept his cloak aside, and to the hostess' unspeakable relief passed out of the door.

"I never knew you," he said in low tones as he went.

The lady murmured some vain excuse about intruders, but the rector stood with annoyance written on his face.

"I beg a thousand pardons," he said to the hostess absently. "It is a great pleasure to be here—somehow I thought I knew that man. I am sure I knew him once."

The stranger had passed down the steps, and as he passed, the nurse, lingering at the top of the staircase, flew down after him, caught his cloak, trembled, hesitated, and then kneeled in the dust.

He touched her lightly with his hand and said: "Go, and sin no more!"

With a glad cry the maid left the house, with its open door, and turned north, running. The stranger turned eastward into the night. As they parted a long, low howl rose tremulously and reverberated through the night. The colonel's wife within shuddered.

"The bloodhounds!" she said.

The rector answered carelessly:

"Another one of those convicts escaped, I suppose. Really, they need severer measures." Then he stopped. He was trying to remember that stranger's name.

The judge's wife looked about for the draft and arranged her shawl. The girl glanced at the white drapery in the hall, but the young officer was bending over her and the fires of life burned in her veins.

Howl after howl rose in the night, swelled, and died away. The stranger strode rapidly along the highway and

out into the deep forest. There he paused and stood waiting, tall and still.

A mile up the road behind a man was running, tall and
powerful and black, with crime-stained face and convicts'
stripes upon him, and shackles on his legs. He ran and
jumped, in little, short steps, and his chains rang. He fell
and rose again, while the howl of the hounds rang louder
behind him.

Into the forest he leapt and crept and jumped and ran,
streaming with sweat; seeing the tall form rise before him,
he stopped suddenly, dropped his hands in sullen impo-
tence, and sank panting to the earth. A greyhound shot out
of the woods behind him, howled, whined, and fawned before the stranger's feet. Hound after hound bayed, leapt,
and lay there; then silently, one by one, and with bowed
heads, they crept backward toward the town.

The stranger made a cup of his hands and gave the man
water to drink, bathed his hot head, and gently took the
chains and irons from his feet. By and by the convict stood
up. Day was dawning above the treetops. He looked into
the stranger's face, and for a moment a gladness swept over
the strains of his face.

"Why, you are a nigger, too," he said.

Then the convict seemed anxious to justify himself.

"I never had no chance," he said furtively.

"Thou shalt not steal," said the stranger.

The man bridled.

"But how about them? Can they steal? Didn't they steal a
whole year's work, and then when I stole to keep from
starving—" He glanced at the stranger.

"No, I didn't steal just to keep from starving. I stole to be
stealing. I can't seem to keep from stealing. Seems like
when I see things, I just must—but, yes, I'll try!"

The convict looked down at his striped clothes, but the stranger had taken off his long coat; he had put it around him and the stripes disappeared.

In the opening morning the black man started toward the low, log arm-house in the distance, while the stranger stood watching him. There was a new glory in the day. The black man's face cleared up, and the farmer was glad to get him. All day the black man worked as he had never worked before. The farmer gave him some cold food.

"You can sleep in the barn," he said, and turned away.

"How much do I git a day?" asked the black man.

The farmer scowled.

"Now see here," said he. "If you'll sign a contract for the season, I'll give you ten dollars a month."

"I won't sign no contract," said the black man doggedly.

"Yes, you will," said the farmer, threateningly, "or I'll call the convict guard." And he grinned.

The convict shrank and slouched to the barn. As night fell he looked out and saw the farmer leave the place. Slowly he crept out and sneaked toward the house. He looked through the kitchen door. No one was there, but the supper was spread as if the mistress had laid it and gone out. He ate ravenously. Then he looked into the front room and listened. He could hear low voices on the porch. On the table lay a gold watch. He gazed at it, and in a moment he was beside it—his hands were on it! Quickly he slipped out of the house and slouched toward the field. He saw his employer coming along the highway. He fled back in terror and around to the front of the house, when suddenly he stopped. He felt the great, dark eyes of the stranger and saw the same dark, cloak-like coat where the stranger sat on the doorstep talking with the mistress of the house. Slowly, guiltily, he turned back, entered the kitchen, and laid the watch stealthily where he had found it; then he rushed wildly back toward the stranger, with arms outstretched.

The woman had laid supper for her husband, and going down from the house had walked out toward a neighbor's. She was gone but a little while, and when she came back she started to see a dark figure on the doorsteps under the tall, red oak. She thought it was the new Negro until he said in a soft voice:

"Will you give me bread?"

Reassured at the voice of a white man, she answered quickly in her soft, Southern tones:

"Why, certainly."

She was a little woman, and once had been pretty; but now her face was drawn with work and care. She was nervous and always thinking, wishing, wanting for something. She went in and got him some cornbread and a glass of cool, rich buttermilk; then she came out and sat down beside him. She began, quite unconsciously, to tell him about herself—the things she had done and had not done and the things she had wished for. She told him of her husband and this new farm they were trying to buy. She said it was hard to get niggers to work. She said they ought all to be in the chain-gang and made to work. Even then some ran away. Only yesterday one had escaped, and another the day before.

At last she gossiped of her neighbors, how good they were and how bad.

"And do you like them all?" asked the stranger.

She hesitated.

"Most of them," she said; and then, looking up into his face and putting her hand into his, as though he were her father, she said:

"There are none I hate; no, none at all."

He looked away, holding her hand in his, and said dreamily:

"You love your neighbor as yourself?"

She hesitated.

"I try—" she began, and then looked the way he was looking; down under the hill where lay a little, half-ruined cabin.

"They are niggers," she said briefly.

He looked at her. Suddenly a confusion came over her and she insisted, she knew not why.

"But they are niggers!"

With a sudden impulse she arose and hurriedly lighted the lamp that stood just within the door, and held it above her head. She saw his dark face and curly hair. She shrieked in angry terror and rushed down the path, and just as she rushed down, the black convict came running up with hands outstretched. They met in mid-path, and before he could stop he had run against her and she fell heavily to earth and lay white and still. Her husband came rushing around the house with a cry and an oath.

"I knew it," he said. "It's that runaway nigger." He held the black man struggling to the earth and raised his voice to a yell. Down the highway came the convict guard, with hound and mob and gun. They paused across the fields. The farmer motioned to them.

"He—attacked—my wife," he gasped.

The mob snarled and worked silently. Right to the limb of the red oak they hoisted the struggling, writhing black man, while others lifted the dazed woman. Right and left, as she tottered to the house, she searched for the stranger with a yearning, but the stranger was gone. And she told none of her guests.

"No—no, I want nothing," she insisted, until they left

her, as they thought, asleep. For a time she lay still, listening to the departure of the mob. Then she rose. She shuddered as she heard the creaking of the limb where the body hung. But resolutely she crawled to the window and peered out into the moonlight; she saw the dead man writhe. He stretched his arms out like a cross, looking upward. She gasped and clung to the windowsill. Behind the swaying body, and down where the little, half-ruined cabin lay, a single flame flashed up amid the far-off shout and cry of the mob. A fierce joy sobbed up through the terror in her soul and then sank abashed as she watched the flame rise. Suddenly whirling into one great crimson column it shot to the top of the sky and threw great arms athwart the gloom until above the world and behind the roped and swaying form below hung quivering and burning a great crimson cross.

She hid her dizzy, aching head in an agony of tears and dared not look, for she knew. Her dry lips moved:

"Despised and rejected of men."

She knew, and the very horror of it lifted her dull and shrinking eyelids. There, heaven-tall, earth-wide, hung the stranger on the crimson cross, riven and bloodstained, with thorn-crowned head and pierced hands. She stretched her arms and shrieked.

He did not hear. He did not see. His calm dark eyes, all sorrowful, were fastened on the writhing, twisting body of the thief, and a voice came out of the winds of the night, saying:

"This day thou shalt be with me in Paradise!"

The Song of the Smoke

I am the Smoke King
I am black!
I am swinging in the sky,
I am wringing worlds awry:
I am the thought of the throbbing mills,
I am the soul of the soul-toil kills,
Wraith of the ripple of trading rills;
Up I'm curling from the sod,
I am whirling home to God;
I am the Smoke King
I am black.

I am the Smoke King,
I am black!
I am wreathing broken hearts,
I am sheathing love's light darts;
Inspiration of iron times
Wedding the toil of toiling climes,
Shedding the blood of bloodless crimes—
Luring lowering 'mid the blue,
Torrid towering toward the true,
I am the Smoke King,
I am black.

I am the Smoke King,
I am black!
I am darkening with song,
I am hearkening to wrong!
I will be black as blackness can—
The blacker the mantle, the mightier the man!
For blackness was ancient ere whiteness began.
I am daubing God in night,

I am swabbing Hell in white:
    I am the Smoke King,
    I am black!
I am cursing ruddy morn,
I am hearsing hearts unborn:
    Souls unto me are as stars in a night,
    I whiten my black men—I blacken my white!
    What's the hue of a hide to man in his might?
Hail! great, gritty, grimy hands—
Sweet Christ, pity toiling lands!
    I am the Smoke King
    I am black.

A Litany of Atlanta

O Silent God, Thou whose voice afar in mist and mystery
    hath left our ears a-hungered in these fearful days—
    Hear us, good Lord!

Listen to us, Thy children: our faces dark with doubt,
    are made a mockery in Thy sanctuary. With uplifted
    hands we front Thy heaven, O God, crying:
    We beseech Thee to hear us, good Lord!

We are not better than our fellows, Lord, we are but weak
    and human men. When our devils do deviltry, curse
    Thou the doer and the deed; curse them as we curse
    them, do to them all and more than ever they have
    done to innocence and weakness, to womanhood and
    home.
    Have mercy upon us, miserable sinners!

And yet whose is the deeper guilt? Who made these
    devils? Who nursed them in crime and fed them on
    injustice? Who ravished and debauched and waxed
    fat and rich on public iniquity?
    Thou knowest, good God!

Is this Thy justice, O Father, that guile be easier than
    innocence, and the innocent crucified for the guilt
    of the untouched guilty?
    Justice, O Judge of men!

Wherefore do we pray? Is not the God of the fathers dead?
    Have not seers seen in Heaven's halls Thine hearsed
    and lifeless form stark amidst the black and rolling

smoke of sin, where all along bow bitter forms of
endless dead?
Awake, Thou that sleepest!

Thou art not dead, but flown afar, up hills of endless light,
thru blazing corridors of suns, where worlds do swing
of good and gentle men, of women strong and free—
far from the cozeage, black hypocrisy and chaste
prostitution of this shameful speck of dust!
Turn again, O Lord, leave us not to perish in our sin!

From lust of body and lust of blood
Great God deliver us!

From lust of power and lust of gold,
Great God deliver us!

From the leagued lying of despot and of brute,
Great God deliver us!

A city lay in travail, God our Lord, and from her loins
sprang twin Murder and Black Hate. Red was the
midnight; clang, crack and cry of death and fury
filled the air and trembled underneath the stars when
church spires pointed silently to Thee. And all this
was to sate the greed of greedy men who hide behind
the veil of vengeance!
Bend us Thine ear, O Lord!

In the pale, still morning we looked upon the deed. We
stopped our ears and held our leaping hands, but
they—did they not wag their heads and leer and cry

with bloody jaws: Cease from crime! The word was
mockery, for thus they train a hundred crimes while
we do cure one.
Turn again our captivity, O Lord!

Behold this maimed and broken thing; dear God it was an
humble black man who toiled and sweat to save a bit
from the pittance paid him. They told him: *Work and
Rise.* He worked. Did this man sin? Nay, but some one
told how some one said another did—one whom he
had never seen nor known. Yet for that man's crime
this man lieth maimed and murdered, his wife naked
to shame, his children, to poverty and evil.
Hear us, O heavenly Father!

Doth not this justice of hell stink in Thy nostrils, O God?
How long shall the mounting flood of innocent
blood roar in Thine ears and pound in our hearts for
vengeance? Pile the pale frenzy of blood-crazed brutes
who do such deeds high on Thine altar, Jehovah Jireh,
and burn it in hell forever and forever!
Forgive us, good Lord; we know not what we say!

Bewildered we are, and passion-tost, mad with the
madness of a mobbed and mocked and murdered
people; straining at the armposts of Thy Throne, we
raise our shackled hands and charge Thee, God, by the
bones of our stolen fathers, by the tears of our dead
mothers, by the very blood of Thy crucified Christ:
What meaneth this? Tell us the Plan: give us the Sign!
Keep not thou silence, O God!

Sit no longer blind, Lord God, deaf to our prayer and
dumb to our dumb suffering. Surely Thou too art
not white, O Lord, a pale, bloodless, heartless thing?
Ah! Christ of all the Pities!

Forgive the thought! Forgive these wild, blasphemous
words. Thou art still the God of our black fathers,
and in Thy soul's soul sit some soft darkenings of
the evening, some shadowings of the velvet night.

But whisper—speak—call, great God, for Thy silence is
white terror to our hearts! The way, O God, show us
the way and point us the path.

Whither? North is greed and South is blood; within, the
coward, and without, the liar. Whither? To death?
Amen! Welcome dark sleep!

Whither? To life? But not this life, dear God, not this.
Let the cup pass from us, tempt us not beyond our
strength, for there is that clamoring and clawing
within, to whose voice we would not listen, yet
shudder lest we must, and it is red, Ah! God!
It is a red and awful shape.
Selah!

In yonder East trembles a star.
Vengeance is mine; I will repay, saith the Lord!

Thy will, O Lord, be done!
Kyrie Eleison!

Lord, we have done these pleading, wavering words.
We beseech Thee to hear us, good Lord!

We bow our heads and hearken soft to the sobbing of
women and little children.
We beseech Thee to hear us, good Lord!

Our voices sink in silence and in night.
Hear us, good Lord!

In night, O God of a godless land!
Amen!

In silence, O Silent God.
Selah!

I Am Resolved

I am resolved *in this New Year to play the man—to stand straight, look the world squarely in the eye, and walk to my work with no shuffle or slouch.*

I am resolved *to be satisfied with no treatment which ignores my manhood and my right to be counted as one among men.*

I am resolved *to be quiet and law abiding, but to refuse to cringe in body or in soul, to resent deliberate insult, and to assert my just rights in the face of wanton aggression.*

I am resolved *to defend and assert the absolute equality of the Negro race with any and all other human races and its divine right to equal and just treatment.*

I am resolved *to be ready at all times and in all places to bear witness with pen, voice, money and deed against the horrible crime of lynching, the shame of "Jim Crow" legislation, the injustice of all color discrimination, the wrong of disfranchisement for race or sex, the iniquity of war under any circumstances and the deep damnation of present methods of distributing the world's work and wealth.*

I am resolved *to defend the poor and the weak of every race and hue, and especially to guard my mother, my wife, my daughter and all my darker sisters from the insults and aggressions of the white men and black, with the last strength of my body and the last suffering of my soul.*

For all these things, I am resolved *unflinchingly to stand, and if this resolve cost me pain, poverty, slander, and even life itself, I will remember the Word of the Prophet, how he sang:*

"Though Love repine and Reason chafe,
   There came a Voice, without reply,
'Tis man's Perdition to be safe
   When for the Truth he ought to die!"

The Three Wise Men

The comet was blazing down from the sky on the midnight before Christmas. Three songs were dying away in the East: one from the rich and ornate chapel of the great cathedral on the hills beyond 110th Street—a song of beauty and exquisite finish but coldly and formally sung. Another, a chant from the dim synagogue on the lower East Side— heavy with droning and passionate; the last from West 53rd Street—a minor wail of utter melody. The songs had died away and three priests, looking at the midnight sky, saw the comet at the same moment. The priest in the ornate chapel, gowned in his silken vestments, paused and stared wonderingly at the star; it seemed drawing near to him and guiding him. Almost before he knew it he had thrown a rich fur cloak about himself and was whirling downtown in a taxicab, watching the star with fascinated gaze. The rabbi on the lower East Side no sooner saw that blaze in the heavens than a low cry of joy left his lips and he followed swiftly, boarding a passing Grand Street car and changing up Broadway; he hung on the footboard to watch unmindful of the gibes at his white beard and Jewish gabardine. The old black preacher of 53rd Street, with sad and wrinkled face, looked at the moving star thoughtfully and walked slowly with it. So the three men threaded the maze of the Christmas-mad streets, neither looking on the surging crowds nor listening to the shouts of the people, but seeing only the star. The "honk, honk" of the priest's taxicab warned the black priest scarcely too soon, and he staggered with difficulty aside as it whizzed by and made the motorman of the car, which bore the Jew, swear at the carelessness of the chauffeur. One flew, the other whirred swiftly and the third walked slowly; yet because of their differing ways they all came to the steps of the great apartment house at the same moment, and they bowed gravely to each other, yet not without curiosity, as each ascended the steps. The porter was strangely deferential and they rose swiftly to the seventh floor, where a wide hall door flew silently open.

Within and before the wide log fire of the drawing room sat a woman. She was tall and shapely and well gowned. She sat alone. The guests had gone an hour since and the last footsteps of the servants were echoing above; yet she sat there weary, still gazing into the mystery of the fire. She had seen many Christmas Eves and they were growing all to be alike—wretchedly alike. All equally lonely, aimless— almost artificial. She arose and walked to the window, sweeping aside the heavy curtains, and the brilliancy of the star blazed in upon her. She looked upon it with a start. She remembered how once long, long years ago she had looked upon stars and such things as very real and shining fingers of fate. She remembered especially on a night like this how some such star had told her future. How out of her soul wonderful things were to be born, and she had said unto the star: "How shall this be?" And something had answered: "That holy thing that shall be born of you shall be called the Son of God." And then she had cried in all her maiden faith and mystery: "Behold the hand-maiden of the Lord, be it according to thy word." And the angel departed from her, and it never came back again. Here she was reaching the portals of middle age with no prospects and few ambitions; to live and wait and sleep; to work a soulless work, to eat in some great manger like this—that was the life that seemed stretching before her endless and without change, until the End and the Change of Changing. And yet she had dreamed such dreams and fancied such fair destiny! As she thought of these dreams to-night a tear gathered and wandered down her face. It was then that she became suddenly aware of two men standing on either side of her, and she felt, but did not see, a third man, who stood behind. But for the soft voice of the first speaker she would have sprung up in alarm, but he was an old man and deferential with soft ascetic Jewish face, with white-forked beard and gabardine, and he bowed in deep humility as he spoke, saying:

"Where is he that is born King of the Jews, for we have seen His star in the East, and have come to worship Him?"

The other surpliced figure, who stood upon her right hand, said the same thing, only less:

"Where is He, for we have seen His star in the East, and have come to worship Him?" And scarcely had his voice ceased than the strong low rolling of another voice came from behind, saying:

"Where is He, for we have seen His star in the East, and have come to worship Him?"

She sank back in her chair and smiled. There was evidently some mistake, and she said to the Jew courteously:

"There is no King here."

"But," said the Jew, eagerly, tremulously, "it is a child we seek, and the star has guided us hither; we have brought gifts of gold and frankincense and myrrh." Still the woman shook her head.

"Children are not allowed in these apartments," she said, "and besides, I am unwed."

"The Scriptures say He shall be born of a Virgin," he chanted. But the woman smiled bitterly.

"The children of Virgins are not welcome in the twentieth century, even though they be Sons of God!"

"And in a manger," continued the Jew.

"This is, indeed, a manger," laughed the woman, "but He is not here—He is not here—only—cattle feed here."

Then the silk-robed priest on the left interrupted:

"You do not understand," he said, "it is not a child of the

body we seek, but of the Word. The Word which was with God and the Word which was God. We seek the illuminating truth which shall settle all our wild gropings and bring light to this blind world." But the woman laughed even more bitterly.

"I was foolish enough once to think," she said, "that out of my brain would leap some wondrous illuminating word which should give light and warmth to the world, but nothing has been born, save here and there an epigram and the smartness of a phrase. No, He is not here."

The surpliced priest drew back with disappointed mien, and then suddenly, in the face of priest and Jew, as they turned toward the unseen figure at her back, she saw the birth of new and wonderful comprehension—Jew and Gentile sank to their knees—and she heard a soft and mighty voice that came up out of the shadows behind her as she bent forward, almost crouching, and it said:

"Him whom we seek is child neither of thy body nor of thy brain, but of thy heart. Strong Son of God, immortal love. We seek not the king of the world nor the light of the world, but the love of the world, and of all men, for all men; and lo! this thou bearest beneath thy heart, O woman of mankind. This night it shall be born!"

Slowly her heart rose and surged within as she struggled to her feet; a wonderful revelation lighted in her whirling brain. She, of all women; she, the chosen one—the bride of Almighty God; her lips babbled noiselessly searching for that old and saintly hymn: "My soul doth magnify the Lord, and my spirit hath rejoiced in God, my saviour. For he hath regarded the low estate of his hand-maiden, for behold! from henceforth all generations shall call me blessed." A great new strength gripped her limbs. Slowly she arose, and as she rose, the roof rose silently with her—the walls of the vast room widened—the cold wet pavement touched her satined feet, and the pale-blue brilliance of the star rained on her coiled hair and naked shoulders. The shouting, careless, noisy midnight crowds surged by and brushed her gown. Slowly she turned herself, with strange new gladness in her heart, and the last words of the hymn on her lips: "He hath put down the Mighty from their seats and hath exalted them of low degree; he hath filled the hungry with good things and the rich he hath sent empty away." She turned, and lo! before her stood that third figure, an old, bent black man, sad faced and pitiful, and yet with brilliant caverned eyes and mighty wings that curved to Heaven. And suddenly there was with the angel a multitude of the heavenly host praising God and saying:

"Glory to God in the highest; and on earth peace, good will toward men."

SELAH!

BIBLIOGRAPHY

Crouch, Stanley, and Playthell, Benjamin. *Reconsidering the Souls of Black Folk: Thoughts on the Groundbreaking Classic Work of W. E. B. Du Bois.* New York: Running Press, 2002.

Du Bois, W. E. B. *Black Reconstruction in America, 1860–1880.* Introduction by David Levering Lewis. New York: Free Press, Simon and Schuster, 1992.

———, and David Levering Lewis. *W. E. B. Du Bois: A Reader.* New York: Henry Holt, 1995.

Fontenot, Chester (ed.); Mary A. Morgan and Sarah Gardner. *W. E. B. Du Bois and Race: Essays Celebrating the Centennial Publication of The Souls of Black Folk.* Macon, Ga.: Mercer University Press, 2001.

Horne, Gerald, and Mary Young (eds.). *W. E. B. Du Bois: An Encyclopedia.* Westport, Conn.: Greenwood Press, 2001.

Lewis, David Levering. *W. E. B. DuBois: Biography of a Race, 1868-1919.* New York: Henry Holt, 1993.

———. *W. E. B. Du Bois: The Fight for Equality and the American Century, 1919–1963.* New York: Henry Holt, 2001.

Wilson, Sondra Kathryn (ed.). *The Crisis Reader.* New York: The Modern Library, Random House, 1999.

INDEX

Burghardt (mother),
15, 18
Du Bois, Nina Gormand
(wife), 15
Du Bois, Shirley Graham
(wife), 15
*Dusk of Dawn: an
Autobiography of a
Concept of Race*
(Du Bois), xv
Duty, 6

Economic history, 124
Education, 59–69
Egypt (Egyptians), 19, 116,
117, 123–24
Emancipation, 41, 47, 97
of labor, 40
of women, 15–19
Emancipation Proclamation,
xi
Encyclopaedia Africana
(Du Bois), xvi, 46
Equality, 33, 40
Ethics, 6
Eugenics, xiii
Evil (evildoing), 6, 7, 123
Evolution, 10
Exploitation (exploited
classes), 7, 35–38

Faith, 6
civilization and, 4
death of, 5
Feminism. *See* Women
Fisk University, 81

Folk customs, 26
"Forty acres and a mule,"
101–2
Founding fathers, 32, 35
slavery and, 108
Fourteenth Amendment, xi
France (French), 76, 77, 85,
87
Freedmen's Bureau, 68
Freedom, 31–42, 50
artists and, 26
sexual, 64
slavery and, 104
Free Negroes, 105, 106–7
Fugitive slaves, 107

Garrison, William Lloyd,
104
Garvey, Marcus, 52
Gates, Henry Louis, Jr., xvi,
46
Germany, 76, 77, 123. *See
also* World War I
Ghana, xv, 32, 116
Gift of Black Folk, The
(Du Bois), xv
Globalization, 11
God. *See also* Religion
slaves and, 105
Gomer, Burghardt, 15
Gondricourt Training
School, 53
Goodness, artists and, 25
Good will, 8
Graham, Shirley, 15
Grandmothers, 18

ABOUT THE EDITOR

Aberjhani is co-author of the *Encyclopedia of the Harlem Renaissance*, and author of the fiction and poetry collection *I Made My Boy of Poetry*. His works have appeared in many magazines and anthologies, including *Essence, Literary Savannah*, and *Sons of Lovers*. A former U.S. Air Force Public Affairs Specialist and Human Relations Counselor, he has traveled extensively throughout the United States and Europe. He often presents recitals and lectures on his work.